FOKKER FODDER

THE ROYAL AIRCRAFT FACTORY B.E.2c

PAUL R. HARE

FONTHILL

Fonthill Media Limited
Fonthill Media LLC
www.fonthillmedia.com
office@fonthillmedia.com

First published in the United Kingdom 2012

British Library Cataloguing in Publication Data:
A catalogue record for this book is available from the British Library

ISBN: 978-1-78155-065-6 (print)
ISBN: 978-1-78155-173-8 (e-book)

Typeset in 10.5pt on 14pt Sabon LT
Printed and bound in England

Connect with us
 facebook.com/fonthillmedia   twitter.com/fonthillmedia

Contents

Acknowledgements

In researching and writing this book I have received help, especially with information or photographs, from many people to each of whom due acknowledgement should be given. These include: the late Jack Bruce, Gerald Burr, Paul Chapman, Mick Davis, Peter Dye, Gene Demarco, Nick Forder, Peter Green, Stuart Howe, Colin Huston, Phil Jarrett, Kevin Kelly, Paul Leaman, Al Lecher, Stuart Leslie, Tim Mason, Leo Opdycke, Andrew Willox, and numerous members of both Cross & Cockade International and WW1 aeroplanes Inc.

However, any mistakes remain, of course, my own.

Paul R. Hare
March 2012

Foreword

Peter Dye OBE, BSc(Eng), MRAeS. ACGI
Air Vice-Marshal RAF (Retired)
Director General – Royal Air Force Museum

As this book makes clear, the B.E.2 was a hugely important aircraft in the story of early British military aviation. Its innovative design ensured wide use throughout the First World War, providing the basis for successive modifications and improvements that (much like the Spitfire in the Second World War) sustained capabilities in line with the growing needs of the frontline. Unlike the Spitfire, however, the B.E.2 was not a glamorous fighter, but an artillery cooperation and reconnaissance machine that carried out the essential and painstaking work of supporting ground operations. It also did many other tasks, ranging from bombing to home defence. Even when its frontline duties ended, the B.E.2 was still to be found in the training schools or operating as a communications aircraft. It is curious, therefore, that the type has earned such a poor reputation. The criticism started during the war, when some of the media, encouraged by campaigning politicians, decided that the Royal Flying Corps was deficient in its administration and that lives were being needlessly lost because of outdated aircraft, notably the B.E.2. These charges were subsequently dismissed, but the mud stuck. In due course, the B.E.2 was replaced in frontline service – not because it was an abject failure but because the rapid advance of technology and the changing needs of the air services demanded a more modern design. Since that time, the B.E.2, although much loved by those that flew it, has become associated with the gallant, but futile, efforts of brave young men sent to war with inadequate equipment and a modest life expectancy.

In truth, the B.E.2 did all that might be reasonably asked of it. As a pre-war design it had no right to still be in service by the Armistice, yet it was. It had no right be to be so successful across so many roles, but it was. It had no right to provide a sound basis for successive improvements over four years of intense air fighting, but it did so. The B.E.2 was a reliable and capable aircraft that gave outstanding service and allowed the Royal Flying Corps to contest, and win, the battle for air superiority against a determined and well equipped opposition. It provided the platform for continued success that ultimately saw the creation of the Royal Air Force. The B.E.2 should be remembered, therefore, with respect and affection, tinged with wonder that a machine designed years before air fighting became a reality could adapt and survive for so long in the maelstrom that was the First World War.

February 2012

Introduction

In the months before and those after the outbreak of the First World War, it was unclear exactly what role aeroplanes would be expected to play in the conflict. Manoeuvres and exercises had confirmed its usefulness for reconnaissance, and some progress had been made with bomb dropping, aerial photography, signalling corrections and with spotting the fall of shot for the artillery. The B.E.2, the single most numerous type in the early Royal Flying Corps, had not only proved itself of value for these various tasks, but had gained numerous other distinctions too, including out-performing the official winner of the 1912 Military Aeroplane Competition.

A B.E.2 had set an altitude record with a passenger at over 10,000 feet and another, fitted with additional fuel tanks, made numerous long-distance flights, including one from Montrose in Scotland to Farnborough via Portsmouth, a distance of well over 500 miles nonstop. The first aerial reconnaissance of the war was carried out by a B.E.2 while, later in the war, B.E.2s shot down more raiding German airships than any other type. It was the only aeroplane to serve with the Royal Flying Corps for all six years of the unit's existence as well as serving both with its predecessor, the Air Battalion of the Royal Engineers, and with its successor, the Royal Air Force.

Developed as the B.E.2c to be inherently stable, the machine would automatically right itself if upset by a gust and so could be flown 'hands off', providing a steady platform from which the crew could more successfully carry out their military duties. This stability is not hard to achieve once the secret is known. (It was achieved by including the correct dihedral angle on the wings by setting the tailplane at a different angle to the mainplanes and by having a sufficient keel area aft of the

The B.E.2 at its most graceful. Two examples of the early version in flight over Farnborough Common, their clear doped fabric seeming almost transparent.

The B.E.2 in its most familiar guise: the inherently stable, unarmed, 90-hp B.E.2c. This example, 8717, was built by Wm. Beardmore & Co. and served with the Royal Navy Air Service at East Fortune, Scotland.

centre of gravity.) Every builder of flying model aeroplanes can do it almost without thinking, but then it was so new and unusual that pilots called the B.E.2c the 'Quirk' because of it.

Naturally, it was thought that aeroplanes would be required to fight, but it was generally assumed that they would do so as soldiers, or even warships do, by swinging their guns around to take aim. Therefore, designers of proposed fighting aeroplanes concentrated on achieving the widest possible field of fire for the gunner by placing him at the front and the engine and propeller at the back. Aeroplanes, it was thought, would fight by exchanging broadsides like Nelson's men of war.

The advent of the true single-seat fighter – in which the gun is fixed and the pilot aims the aeroplane at his opponent – was initially not considered feasible. However, such a concept was introduced in 1915 by the French and with far greater success by Germany. The B.E.2 was instantly outclassed, its stability now a liability and losses escalated as the number of enemy fighters, principally Fokker monoplanes, grew. With fatalistic humour, the crews of the B.E.2 referred to themselves and their mounts as 'Fokker Fodder' as they continued to engage, like lambs to the slaughter, in a form of warfare for which the B.E.2 had never been designed.

By 1916, the situation was such that one outspoken Member of Parliament openly accused the War Office of murdering its crews by sending them out to fly in such a defenceless machine. It is for this, rather than its numerous other achievements and many successes, that the B.E.2 is chiefly remembered today.

It deserves better.

Background

The British Army first formally embraced aviation in 1878 when James Templer, an officer of the 2nd Middlesex Militia, was awarded an allowance of £150 with which to construct an observation balloon, a move entirely typical of the self-sufficient Victorian military. Templer, who was an enthusiastic and experienced sporting balloonist, completed the task well within budget producing a 10,000-cubic-feet-capacity hydrogen balloon aptly named 'Pioneer' for just £71. Templer went on to oversee production at the H. M. Balloon Factory, first based at Chatham and later Aldershot, to build many more military balloons before advancing, in the early years of the twentieth century, in the construction of an airship. Both assembling and operating such a vessel required far more space than the balloon factory's cramped quarters could provide. Therefore, a move was made in 1905 to relocate to a new site on the northern edge of Farnborough Common where the facility remained, through several changes of name, for almost a century.

Operation of the balloons was in the hands of a separate unit of the Royal Engineers named the Balloon School. In 1904, its Commanding Officer, Colonel Capper, returned from a visit to the US where he studied exhibits relating to advances in aviation and was full of enthusiasm for the aeroplane recently invented by the Wright Brothers. However, for a variety of reasons, negotiations for the purchase of an aeroplane from the Wrights dragged on sporadically for some years until Capper – who had succeeded Templer as superintendent of the factory in 1906 – decided that the Army should remain self-sufficient and the Balloon Factory should build their own. Two separate design philosophies were explored: a swept wing design produced by John W. Dunne and a large pusher, very loosely based on the Wright Brothers design, by Samuel

The Royal Aircraft Factory at Farnborough, home of the B.E.2, with aeroplane workshops to the right and original airship shed behind them.

A Cody man-lifting kite with its inventor, in sombrero, at the right of the picture. It was his invention of these kites that brought S. F. Cody into the service of the British Army where he would eventually, on 16 October 1908, make the first powered flight in England.

Mervyn O'Gorman, the gifted engineer who developed the Royal Aircraft Factory in to the foremost aeronautical research establishment in the world, seen in his Chelsea home.

Franklin Cody. At the time, Cody was employed by the British Army to instruct in the operation of man-lifting kites of his own devising.

By the beginning of 1909, success was still evading Dunne, and although Cody had succeeded in making the first officially recognised powered flight in England the previous October, this had ended in a crash causing extensive damage to which repairs had yet to be completed. Therefore, Mr R. B. Haldane, Secretary of State for War, whose reforms were sweeping through the British Army, bought the experiments upon which the sum of £2,500 had so far been expended, to an end, discharging both Cody and Dunne, and returning Capper to the Balloon School. In his place at the Balloon Factory, he engaged Mervyn O'Gorman, a civilian consulting engineer, hoping that a scientific approach to solving the problems of flight would bring greater success. At the same time, Haldane restricted the activities of the factory to building such balloons and airships as the War Office required. Also, the factory was to repair and maintain any aeroplanes that the Army might acquire, and to conduct aeronautical research.

On 10 October 1910, it was announced that the scope of the Royal Engineers was to be increased to 'afford opportunities for aeroplaning', a move that helped to further the Balloon Factory's involvement with aeroplanes, although without yet allowing it to create new designs without express authority. Such authority was rarely given and restricted both the Factory's experimental programme and the growth of the military air services. The aeroplanes acquired were bought piecemeal, and since at the time no one knew what was required of a military aeroplane, no design was too bizarre to be considered. Towards the end of 1910, Geoffrey de Havilland had completed building and testing his first successful aeroplane, and with funds exhausted, was uncertain of his next step. Following an interview with O'Gorman at his Chelsea home, de Havilland was offered a job at the Balloon Factory as a designer/test pilot and managed to sell his aeroplane, a fairly conventional pusher design, to his new employers for £400 thus ensuring that he would have an aeroplane to test. Following extensive research, O'Gorman defined all existing aeroplanes in three groups or classes based upon their layout and how they achieved stability in pitch. These were: Class B – Tractor designs with the propeller at the front and tailplane at the rear. Named for the Bleriot. Other contemporary examples were the Avro, Antoinette and Breguet; Class F – Pusher designs with the propeller behind the wings and tailplane at the rear. Examples were the Farman from which the group was named and the Bristol Boxkite; and Class S – Canard designs with the stabilising

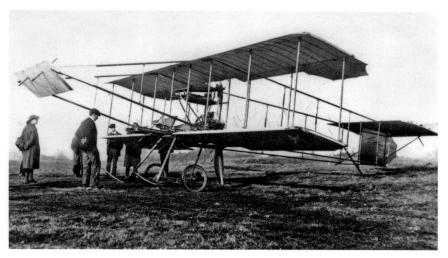

Geoffrey de Havilland's first successful design, adopted by the Royal Aircraft Factory as F.E.1. It underwent a great deal of modification and development during its career.

The S.E.1 which, despite constant development, failed to live up to the expectations that its design had shown on paper.

surface in front and propeller at the rear. Named for the Santos-Dumont 14 bis, another example being the Valkyrie. De Havilland's machine fell into Class F and was therefore designated Farman Experimental No. 1 or F.E.1, and experimental work, and development of the design kept de Havilland busy during the first months of 1911.

In April that year, the Air Battalion, Royal Engineers, came into being, formalising the Army's experiments with aeroplanes that had previously been conducted with a handful of privately owned machines. At the same time, the Balloon Factory was renamed as the Army Aircraft Factory, more accurately covering its works on balloons, kite and aeroplanes, although its functions remained strictly as before. The arrival of a Bleriot XII for repair gave de Havilland further design work as O'Gorman managed to persuade the War Office to allow some reconstruction within the repairs. What emerged from the workshop in June 1911 was a completely new machine, the tractor monoplane transformed into a canard biplane, the S.E.1. Trials revealed valuable information on handling characteristics of the type and the need for a number of modifications. It was still undergoing development when, on 18 August, the Factory's assistant superintendent, Theodore Ridge, insisted against de Havilland's advice on flying it. Unfortunately, he crashed while attempting a turn causing fatal injuries and wrecking the machine.

B.E.1

Having conducted trials of both F and S classes of aeroplane, the Army Aircraft Factory was keen to test a Class B machine to complete the comparison. Their opportunity came when an out of date Voisin pusher, which in May 1911 had been presented to the newly formed Air Battalion, crashed and was sent to the factory for repair. O'Gorman therefore again employed the 'reconstruction' ruse and wrote on 1 August 1911 to his superior at the War Office, the Director of Fortifications and Works, as follows:

> With reference to the Voisin aeroplane recently presented by the Duke of Westminster and delivered to this Factory by the Wolseley Tool and Motor Co., I have to report that the method of controlling and steering this machine is obsolete and different from any present make; that the wood frame of the wings and struts and the canvas covering have deteriorated to such a degree that they should be replaced if the machine is to be flown in safety.
>
> I therefore desire to recommend that I may be instructed to fit this machine with certain spare wings and struts that I have in stock and alter the control so that it is similar to the Farman type, and thus enable the machine to be flown by anyone qualified to fly a Farman type machine.
>
> I am in a position to effect these alterations quickly and economically and it would then be equal to a good Farman type machine.

Of course, the Army Aircraft Factory had no spare wings or struts in stock and initially planned to reuse the Voisin wings, suitably recovered, in the rebuilt machine. However, the wings, which lacked any form of lateral control and had their main spars at the leading edge, were quickly discarded, but not before their lower root fittings had been incorporated

A Voisin pusher similar to the one from which B.E.1 was 'reconstructed'. Any similarity between the two machines is entirely imaginary, only the engine was reused.

into the new machine. As a means of circumventing the restriction on the creation of new designs, the request served its purpose admirably and official approval was given on 12 August.

Design of the reconstructed machine was entrusted to de Havilland under the supervision of F. M. Green, the Factory's chief engineer. During the machine's development, O'Gorman produced the following statement as part of a presentation to the Advisory Committee for Aeronautics (of which he was an enthusiastic member) that was published as part of Report and Memorandum No. 59 entitled 'Experiments with Full Size Aeroplanes':

1] Lateral control is to be obtained by warping a very large portion of both top and bottom planes, instead of warping a small portion, This is both more powerful and more efficient.

2] A new form of landing chassis is to be designed with adequate provision for absorbing vertical shocks by means of oil buffers and pneumatic absorbers.

3] Provision is to be made for steering the machine on the ground at slow speeds by means of a swivelling skid placed back under the tail. (This facilitates landing in a restricted area.)

16

4] The motor and propeller to be placed in front of the planes to give the pilot a better chance in case of a bad smash. The pilot is raised sufficiently above the bottom plane so that he gets a good view of the ground over the front edge of the bottom plane. This is inferior to the view in the S.E.1 but at least as good as any other aeroplane with the engine in front.

5] The main surfaces are to be placed well in front of the machine and the stabilising surfaces at the rear set at a considerably smaller angle. This will ensure fore and aft stability, but I incline to retain some curvature in the upper surface of the tail as giving a better riding moment.

6] The rudder, and covered body will, I think, ensure sufficient directional stability. It is a matter of trial whether an extra vertical fin be fitted, and in any case this is very easy to do.

7] It is proposed to use a small amount of dihedral angle between the planes, probably 178 degrees, i.e. 1 degree rise on each half plane.

8] The section of the planes of the new machine will not be dissimilar to those of S.E.1

9] The general construction of the machine will be improved considerably in detail, particularly with regard to the planes. Streamlined section struts are being used, and the main stay wires will be swaged to a streamline section. Every effort is being made to reduce head resistance as much as possible.

B.E.1, the first of a long series, its relatively quiet engine earning it the name of 'The Silent Aeroplane'.

In fact, neither the pneumatic undercarriage nor the streamline wires were included in the completed machine, yet it was a very advanced design for its day.

The B.E.1 was a two-bay tractor biplane, the upper wing of slightly greater span than the lower, rigged with neither stagger nor dihedral. Lateral control was by warping the whole wing structure with a tall control column intended to keep stick forces to a minimum. The fuselage was built in two halves joined with fishplates behind the rear cockpit, the forward portion having sturdy lower longerons to carry the undercarriage and the rear portion being a tapering box section, ply covered on the top and bottom and wire braced at the sides. The front passenger cockpit was positioned at the centre of gravity, thus avoiding trim changes if the machine was flown solo. The seat was of wicker as would become standard, but the pilot's seat was moulded from plywood. The forward fuselage was covered in aluminium sheet, the rear in fabric, while formers and stringers gave the fabric-covered top decking of the rear fuselage an elegant curved surface. Formers and a single stringer gave a slight curve to the fabric covering the cockpit sides, slightly increasing the space within the rather narrow fuselage. There was no decking between the cockpits which, although very open and exposed to modern eyes, were considered sufficiently well protected against the elements by the standards of the day. The only instrument fitted appears to have been a direct drive revolution counter mounted on a rear centre section strut for the undivided cockpit allowed no space for an instrument board and the designer obviously saw no immediate need for one. A step was provided to assist the pilot to climb into the cockpit; however, although it has long been customary to mount an aeroplane like a horse from the left side, the step was positioned on the starboard side of the fuselage.

A large aerofoil section tailplane was mounted directly on the upper longerons and an ear-shaped rudder was hinged from an un-braced stern post. Both rudder and elevators were formed around frames of steel tube, fitted with ribs to maintain the correct cross section and fabric covered. The undercarriage had long skids designed to help protect the propeller when the tail was raised for take-off/landing and the sprung tailskid was arranged to swivel so as to improve handling on the ground.

The 60-hp Wolesley V8 engine, recovered from the damaged Voisin, was mounted on tubular bearers, the forward ends of which provided

Geoffrey de Havilland crouching to examine the undercarriage of B.E.1. The step that assisted entry into the cockpit is in front of his face.

a mounting for the anti-drift wires bracing the wings and was covered with an aluminium cowling. As the engine was water-cooled, the radiator was mounted on brackets fixed to the forward centre section struts, adversely affecting the forward view but ensuring the most efficient cooling possible. A blind was provided to blank off the upper part of the radiator to avoid over-cooling in cold weather. Long exhaust pipes passed through the fuselage, terminating below the fuselage, aft of the cockpits, and incorporated car-type attenuators whose efficiency caused the new machine to be dubbed 'The Silent Army Aeroplane' by the press. The main fuel tank was fitted under the passenger seat, a cylindrical gravity tank with conical ends suspended below the upper centre section to feed fuel to the carburettor that was kept warm by the close proximity of the exhaust pipes. Two propellers were bolted together at right angles to form the four-blade unit that would become a familiar feature of Factory designs.

B.E.1 made its first flight, piloted by its designer Geoffrey de Havilland, on 4 December 1911. However, the trial, for which de Havilland claimed just 2/6 in flying pay, was cut short as the engine would not respond to the throttle and the carburettor was therefore replaced with a Claudel unit. This proved effective, despite the engine still not achieving its rated

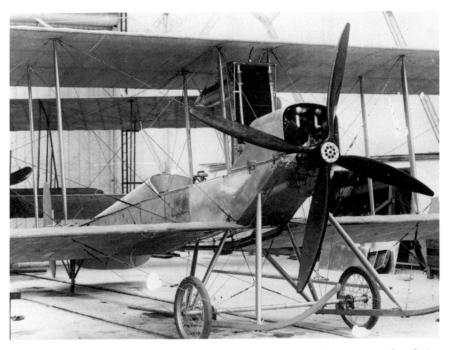

B.E.1 in the Farnborough workshops, apparently completed and awaiting its first flight. (*Crown Copyright*)

revolutions, and numerous subsequent flights were made, many with a passenger.

The Times newspaper in reporting some of these flights commented that:

> The machine is fitted with an eight cylinder Wolseley engine giving from 50 to 60 horsepower, and during a flight last evening could not be heard 50 yards away.

Flight magazine reported on the flights too, praising the new machine and also commenting on its quietness:

> The machine ... is a large biplane with an absolutely silent engine. It has been said that it is a remodelled version of the Duke of Westminster's old Voisin, but it seem to us that there was more remodelling than anything else, and everything that one could see about the machine was of singular interest.

The detail construction also gives evidence of extreme care, and the application of the principle of streamline form together with the complete absence of visible rigging wires in the tail are both points worthy of comment.

On 12 January, a 'Zenith' carburettor was installed but proved less flexible than the original and the Claudel was refitted the following day. Development included moving the wheels back to reduce the weight on the tailskid and thus shorten the take-off run, and re-rigging the wings with three inches of negative stagger as the machine proved slightly tail heavy. Later, a larger tailplane was fitted, presumably to address the same problem. One degree of dihedral was also rigged into the main planes to aid lateral stability as included in O'Gorman's original description. Constant adjustments and modifications were made to the engine and carburettor in order to reach the 1,200 rev/min at which the manufacturer's rating had been achieved, 1,175 being the best obtained.

Once development was complete, the Royal Aircraft Factory had no further reason to retain the machine that was officially a rebuilt version of the Army's Voisin and, on 11 March 1912, it was handed over to the Air Battalion for service use. Three days later, Mr S. Heckstall-Smith, the Factory's assistant superintendent, issued the following document:

B.E.1 CERTIFICATE

This is to certify that the aeroplane B.E.1 has been thoroughly tested by me, and that the mean speed over a ¾ mile course with a live load of 25 stone and sufficient petrol for one hour's flight is 58-59 m.p.h.

The rate of rising loaded as above has been tested up to 600 feet and found to be at the rate of 155 feet per minute.

The machine has been inverted and suspended from the centre and the wings loaded to three times the normal loading. On examination after this test the aeroplane showed no sign of defect.

In April 1912, the Air Battalion became part of the newly formed Royal Flying Corps and B.E.1 was given the serial B7, later changed to 201. It was mostly flown by Major C. J. Burke, an early enthusiast for military aviation whose bulky figure earned him the nickname of 'Pregnant Percy'. Lt John Mackwood, a pilot under Burke's command, later recalled:

The Major showed me his machine, the first B.E in existence, compared with other types this was an excellent affair. It had warping wings, a covered in fuselage and wheel with skids to prevent its turning over. It could do something over sixty miles an hour. Naturally the Major used it himself.

In June, the B.E.1 was returned to what was now renamed the Royal Aircraft Factory where its engine was replaced with a 60-hp Renault V8, but which, being air-cooled, eliminated the radiator and its pipework, thus reducing drag and improving the forward view. A scoop was fitted above the engine to improve the flow of cooling air and a blanking plate closed the vee between the cylinder banks to ensure that the air flow passed around the cylinders. At some point it was provided with decking between the cockpits to improve crew comfort. It was slightly damaged on 10 February 1913 when its engine failed when flown cross-country by Captain Darbyshire who force-landed in fog in Regent's Park. The B.E.1, 201, which had nosed over causing damage to its undercarriage and propeller, was dismantled and returned to Farnborough by road for the necessary repairs to be carried out. During its long career, it served with 2, 4 and 5 Squadrons before ending up at the Central Flying School in Upavon. Its presence is last recorded on 21 September 1916 by which time it had been fitted with a 70-hp engine and a later model fuselage. It had become, in the words of the official historian, '...the revered grandfather of the whole brood of factory aeroplanes'. As such perhaps it should have been preserved but, with the First World War in progress, the authorities had more pressing matters to consider and no steps were taken to ensure its continued existence. Its eventual fate is unknown.

B.E.2

By the end of January 1912, B.E.1 had been joined by a sister ship that was identical in every way to B.E.1 except that it was powered by a Renault engine. The engine mounting tubes were slightly longer so that it was mounted slightly further forwards, moving the centre of gravity and reducing the tail heaviness. Also, it was fitted with a four-blade propeller. This turned at half-engine speed as, in the Renault design, was mounted on an extensive of the camshaft drive rather than directly on the crankshaft.

The new machine was designated B.E.2, not because it was a new design, but simply to denote it as the second machine built in the B Class. Only later, when the design entered volume production did B.E.2 become a type classification since the drawings issued to manufacturers bore that designation, although O'Gorman in his diary referred to the new machine as a 'Military Biplane of the B.E.1 Type', logically considering the earlier machine as the prototype.

B.E.2 was never passed off as being anything but a new machine, copied from B.E.1., without any 'reconstruction' ruse to account for its existence. However, permission to build it appears to have only been obtained retrospectively, for as late as 26 January 1912 when it was virtually complete, O'Gorman included it a memo to the War Office entitled 'Suggested Aeroplanes for Construction'.

De Havilland took B.E.2 up for its initial flight at 11.00 am on 1 February making a total of four flights, including one with F. M. Green, the Factory's chief engineer, as a passenger, covering a total of twenty miles and noting that it seemed faster than its predecessor. The new machine performed perfectly without the need for any modification, all the necessary development work having been done with B.E.1. Although

Geoffrey de Havilland seated in the original B.E.2 outside the flight sheds on Farnborough Common. The wings are of equal span.

from then on, de Havilland largely concentrated his efforts on the new machine, leaving flying of B.E.1 to his new assistant, E. W. Copeland Perry. B.E.2 was later described by *Flight* magazine as being:

> One of the neatest biplanes ever built, and one moreover that impresses the engineering sense with an immediate satisfaction in the quality of the design.

The same article also stated:

> ...it is difficult to describe in words the precise quality of the design that calls forth the admiration of the engineer, and it is certainly not in any way due to the smart finish of superficial details, although the workmanship is excellent, the hand of the experimenter is on it still. The fact remains, that for a well designed tractor biplane, the B.E.2 of the R.A.F. is hard to beat, and some points in it may well be worth copying by those in search of Army orders.

On 5 February, B.E.2 was proudly shown to members of the Advisory Committee for Aeronautics who were paying a visit to the Royal Aircraft Factory. De Havilland made numerous short flights in it during the next few weeks, not to carry out specific tests, but to give air experience to senior Factory design staff. Towards the end of February, de Havilland, accompanied by Green, flew it to Brooklands attracting further favourable comments from the press, *Flight* magazine commenting:

> ...unfortunately it was, in two senses, a flying visit, for the machine departed before everyone had a chance to examine it. It did, however, create a very favourable impression, its finish, workmanship, and climbing power leaving all being considered praiseworthy.

Without having to hand B.E.2 over to the Air Battalion or the Royal Flying Corps, the Factory made the most of their aeroplane. It was retained at Farnborough and became the subject of a number of tests and trials.

In March, it was fitted with a wireless transmitter developed by Mr R. Widdington, aerials for which were fixed along the leading edges of the wings. Trials began on 26 March when four flights were made before the apparatus broke down. With the wireless repaired, tests resumed and continued until 11 April with a number of different operators, its signals being clearly received at ranges of two miles. During these experiments, B.E.2 took part in the first wireless-controlled artillery shoot, shaping the way for its future role.

By 22 April, B.E.2 had flown over twenty hours, covering 1,350 miles and the engine was replaced with another Renault, up-rated to 70 hp by increasing the bore from 90 to 96 mm. This, unusually for the Factory, had been purchased new, demonstrating just how important the B.E.2 was considered to be. Although 23 lbs heavier, the new engine was otherwise little different from its predecessor, the only changes to the installation were a slightly taller air scoop and the exhaust pipes re-routed to run outside the fuselage. Although brackets were provided for them, there is no evidence that the silencers, which had caused so much interest on B.E.1, were fitted to its sister ship. The engine change was completed on 28 April when de Havilland took it up for a brief test flight finding everything satisfactory.

The extra power was to prove useful for the next experiment in which B.E.2 was fitted with floats. On 11 May, de Havilland flew it to Fleet

Close-up of B.E.2 in the Farnborough workshops. As built, the exhaust pipes run through the fuselage. The bulbous object fixed on the starboard side of the cockpit is a direct-drive rev counter. (*Crown Copyright*)

Pond, the largest body of water in the area, and the floats that had been brought by road were fitted. After some adjustments to the machine's balance, and to cope with the shallowness of the pond, a take-off was made towards evening and the machine flew successfully. However, the floats, and possibly the aeroplane, were damaged during the landing and B.E.2 was left in situ for repairs, Perry flying it back to Farnborough on 14 May. The experiment had proved its point and there were no further attempts to fit the B.E.2 with floats although trials continued with other types.

During the next few weeks, B.E.2 was flown to test a thrust meter, and on 31 May, flew with a tension meter fitted to the warp wires, collecting experimental data to aid the Factory's programme of research all of which was later published by the Advisory Committee for Aeronautics. Later the same day, de Havilland, flying solo, climbed to over 6,000 feet in just fifteen minutes, probably the greatest height the type had thus far obtained. B.E.2 was also used to test an accelerometer and the 'Trajectograph', an instrument designed by the Factory for use in the forthcoming Aeroplane Competition that combined an altimeter with a timing device and so measured glide angle.

Many of these trials were reported not only in aviation magazines but in the national press as the following paragraph from *The Times* for 4 June illustrates:

> An experiment in bomb dropping was carried out at Farnborough last evening by Mr de Havilland, of the Army (sic) Aircraft Factory. The 'bomb' carried was an ordinary ringed square weight of 112lb, which was suspended by a trigger hook to the chassis of Army biplane B.E.2. Mr de Havilland detached the weight at a height of about 200 feet. The release had no perceptible effect upon the flight or equilibrium of the biplane.

On 19 June, in a brief departure from his official duties, de Havilland took his wife for a brief joyride in B.E.2, the first time she had flown. What greater endorsement of the comfort and safety of the design, and of its designer's confidence in it could there have possibly been?

Military Aeroplane Competition

Following the formation of the Air Battalion in April 1911, the British aeroplane industry expected to receive orders from the War Office for new machines with which they expected the unit to be equipped. However, they were to be disappointed when what few new aeroplanes were acquired were largely built in France. When the French Army announced that it was to hold a competition to find the most suitable aeroplanes to equip its own air service, pressure was put on the British Government for it to do the same. Towards the end of 1911, it was finally announced that such a competition would be held in the summer of 1912. In addition to the cash prizes on offer, the entrants hoped to sell sufficient examples of the winning design to equip an air force. Together with the list of prizes on offer, the following performance specification was published to which O'Gorman had contributed:

SPECIFICATION FOR A MILITARY AEROPLANE

The following conditions are those required to be fulfilled by a military aeroplane:

1] Delivered in a packing case suitable for transport by rail not exceeding 32ft by 9ft by 9ft. The case must be fitted with eyebolts to facilitate handling.

2] Carry a live load of 350 lbs. in addition to its equipment of instruments etc., with fuel and water for 4 1/2 hours.

3] Fly for three hours loaded as in Clause 2 and maintain an altitude of 4,500 ft. for one hour, the first 1,000ft. being attained at the rate of 200ft. a minute, although a rate of rise of 300 ft a minute is desirable.

4] Attain a speed of not less than 55 m.p.h. in a calm, loaded as in Clause 2.

5] Plane down to ground in a calm from not more than 1,000 ft. with the engine stopped, during which time a horizontal distance of not less than 6,000 ft. must be traversed before touching.

6] Rise without damage from long grass, clover, or harrowed land in 100 yards, in a calm, loaded as in Clause 2.

7] Land without damage on any cultivated ground, including rough plough, in a calm, loaded as in Clause 2, and pull up within 75 yards of the point at which it first touches the ground when landing on smooth turf in a calm. It must be capable of being steered when running slowly on the ground.

8] Be capable of change from flying trim to road transport trim, and travel either on its own wheels, or on a trolley on the road; width not to exceed 10 ft.

9] Provide accommodation for a pilot and observer, and the controls must be capable of use either by pilot or observer.

Further;-

10] The pilot's and observer's view of the country below them to front and flanks must be as open as possible, and they should be shielded from wind and able to communicate with one another.

11] All parts of the aeroplane must be strictly interchangeable, like parts with one another and with spares from stock.

Parts of this specification were clearly based on the performance of the B.E.1, although some improvements, particularly in rate of climb were anticipated. The choice of 55 mph for the required speed seems slow until it is considered that B.E.1 had only achieved 59 mph and O'Gorman then had no way of knowing whether the B.E.2 might do better. On 26 January 1912, O'Gorman issued a memo to the War Office suggesting certain experimental aeroplanes which he thought should be built included the following:

B.E.2 – Military trials biplane of the B.E.1 type
This aeroplane should be put in hand as soon as possible as it should be used as a standard of excellence for the competition machines. It is intended that this machine should fulfil all the conditions laid down as necessary and desirable and shall have a speed considerably in excess of that stipulated.

The memo, dated a few days before the completed machine emerged, clearly illustrates that O'Gorman confidently expected it to be at least as good as any machine entered. However, the B.E.2 was not allowed to compete as O'Gorman, as Superintendent of the Royal Aircraft Factory,

Geoffrey de Havilland and F. H. Sykes in the B.E.2 in which they gained the altitude record of 10,560 feet.

was one of the judges, along with Brigadier-General David Henderson, Captain Godfrey Paine RN (Commandant of the Central Flying School) and Major Frederick H. Sykes (O C Military Wing, RFC).

On 3 February, just two days after its first flight, de Havilland flew the B.E.2 with a total load of 350 lbs and fuel for a four-and-a-half hour flight, exactly as required by the competition rules in order to check that its rate of climb was over 200 feet per minute, a figure the Wolseley-powered B.E.1 had been unable to achieve. Fortunately, the B.E.2 exceeded all expectations and would be further improved by the 70-hp engine fitted before the trials began.

A total of thirty-two entries were officially entered, but when the competition commenced, the first day was the wettest and windiest August on record and a number of aeroplanes failed to arrive at Larkhill on Salisbury Plain to take part. A minor accident, in late July, in which B.E.2 collided with another aircraft may have prevented it taking part in the competition. Nevertheless, de Havilland flew B.E.2 on 8 August and completed the performance tests so as to provide a comparison with the official entrants as it had been designed to do.

Another view of B.E.2, again with de Havilland and Sykes onboard.

On the morning of 12 August with Sykes as a passenger, de Havilland climbed B.E.2 as high as it might possible go. On his return to Larkhill, the barograph carried onboard for the occasion gave an accurate reading of 10,560 feet, thus establishing a record.

In addition to completing the performance tests and securing the altitude record, de Havilland appears to have used B.E.2 as a general runabout as the following quotation from *The Morning Post* illustrates:

> Indeed, throughout the period of the Trials we have seen this machine daily being used for carrying messages, delivering parcels, taking observers to particular coigns of vantage at faster speed than could be possible by any motor car, and in general giving the best illustration yet afforded of what manner of thing a latter day, middle sized, flying machine can be for practical service.

Flight magazine noted that de Havilland also provided a taxi service for officials and favoured members of the press:

> And there stands B.E.2 quietly on the grass in the next field, inviting a ride. "Will you take me back to the sheds De Havilland, while Major Sykes is busy

The second example of the Cody design that won the Military Aeroplane Competition. Despite its success, it was unsuitable for military purposes.

talking to Gen. Henderson?" I ask, and, "Yes, certainly, but you may find it bumpy," says G.de H, putting on his flying cap and goggles, while I clamber into the front seat, a wicker basket affair that seems uncommonly comfortable. Going to the propeller, De Havilland gives it a pull round, as one would start a motor car engine, and the 70 hp Renault gets gently into action...

Opening the throttle a little we turn round into position and accelerate down wind. No bump of any description come to indicate whether or not we are still in contact with the earth, but it is quite certain a moment later that we are flying as with a quiet but determined stride the machine steps into the air.

And now the sheds are just in front so De Havilland puts round into the wind on a small bank and we glide downwards with a smooth easy motion that appeals to me as the most exhilarating part of the flight. At the last moment a skilful movement of the elevator flattens out the machine so that it flies parallel to the ground and a second later the wheels touch the grass and we come to rest on terra firma once more.

Of all the events in the trials nothing impressed me more than this simple flying to and fro.

B.E.2 being prepared for the Aeronautical Exhibition at Olympia in February 1913.

However, rather more than flying to and fro was required to impress the judges who were interested only in facts and figures, carefully measured and recorded. When these were finally gathered and compiled, it was announced that the competition had been won by Cody flying a development of the pusher design that had made the first flight at Farnborough four years before. Not only did the archaic design score very highly on such tests as the field of view from the pilot's seat and the shortness of its landing run, but, as it was powered by a massive Austro-Daimler engine developing 120 hp, it managed an impressive top speed too. Cody was awarded the maximum prize of £5,000 in addition to which the War Office, in accordance with the rules, purchased the machine and ordered another like it. The War Office had begun the competition rather unsure as to what qualities a military aeroplane should possess. At the end of the competition, they were still uncertain, but it was obvious whatever those qualities were, the Cody machine did not have them.

However, a comparison of the results obtained shows that the B.E.2 not only beat Cody, except in maximum speed where its comparatively low power put it at a disadvantage, but often bettered the best results achieved by any competitor.

Test	Cody	B.E.2	Best Result
Maximum speed	72.4 mph	70 mph	75.4 mph (Hanriot No. 2)
Lowest speed	48.5 mph	40 mph	37.4 mph (M. Farman)
Speed range	23.9 mph	30 mph	23.9 mph (Cody)
Climb	288 ft/min	365 ft/min	364 ft/min (Hanriot No. 1)
Glide angle	1 in 6.2	1 in 6.25	1 in 6.8 (M. Farman)
Range	336 miles	420 miles	400 miles (Hanriot No. 1)

Obviously, the B.E.2 was the superior aeroplane overall. Also, those responsible for providing aeroplanes for the Royal Flying Corps could clearly see it and so, as well as placing orders for other machines, most notably the Maurice Farman that had performed well in the trials, placed orders for the Royal Aircraft Factory design. Both Cody's winning machine and the B.E.2 were exhibited in the Aero Show at Olympia from 14 to 22 February 1913.

The Range Extends

During 1911 and early 1912, de Havilland undertook several further designs including B.E.3 and B.E.4, which were rotary-powered machines employing wings of similar planform to the B.E.1, but were otherwise of a completely different design.

B.E.7 was a single-seat variant of the same design and B.E.8 a return to the two-seat layout powered by a 80-hp rotary engine, a number being manufactured by contractors and serving with the Royal Flying Corps. It shared the same wings and vertical tail surfaces as the B.E.2, but not the same flying characteristics and was nicknamed 'the Bloater'.

In the creation of B.E.5, the 'reconstruction' subterfuge was again employed, the donor aircraft being the ill-fated S.E.1 whose 60-hp

The original B.E.3 with its designer, Geoffrey de Havilland, seated in the cockpit. As can be seen, the differences between it and the B.E.2 were fairly extensive.

The rotary-powered B.E.8, developed from the B.E.3, employed some B.E.2 components but was a completely different machine.

ENV engine was reused in a new machine that was otherwise virtually identical to B.E.2, although its wings were of equal span. As the engine was water-cooled, a radiator was fitted by means of metal brackets to the forward centre section struts exactly as had been done in B.E.1. As the machine was now fitted with a Renault engine that was air-cooled, it is possible that it was even the same radiator. Piloted by de Havilland, B.E.5 made its first flight on 27 June 1912 and proved to be trouble free. By 15 July, the B.E.5 was in service with No. 2 Squadron, the Royal Flying Corps finally receiving a replacement to the Bleriot, which had originally provided the ENV engine over a year earlier.

On 22 July, B.E.5 was damaged on landing while flown by Lt Cockrell and ended up on its nose and was returned to the Factory for repairs where it was fitted with new wings of unequal span. During repairs, the engine was changed to that of a 60-hp Renault recovered from an obsolete Breguet, making it identical to a production B.E.2, as it came to be regarded. It was returned to the Royal Flying Corps in good time to take part in the autumn manoeuvres and given the serial 205.

The B.E.5. Once it had been fitted with a Renault engine, as seen here, it was indistinguishable from a B.E.2.

Transferred to No. 3 Squadron, it continued in service until mid-November when it was returned to the factory to be fitted with a 70-hp engine. In May 1913, it was transferred back to No. 2 Squadron, now stationed at Montrose in Scotland and was ferried north by Major Burke, the journey taking several days. Early in the morning of 27 May, 205 was flown by Lt Desmond Arthur who, after thirty minutes in perfect weather, was descending from 2,000 feet in a gliding turn when the upper right wing broke up, bringing the machine down near the railway station at Lunan Bay. The pilot may have unfastened his seat belt and jumped clear before the crash, landing about 100 yards from the wrecked aeroplane. His terrible injuries included a broken neck, death therefore being instantaneous. Following a funeral service at St Mary's Episcopal Church in Montrose, he was buried with full military honours in the aptly named Sleepyhillock Cemetery. An enquiry established that the crash had been caused by the failure of a repair to the rear spar of the top right-hand wing about eleven inches from the tip, which had initiated the collapse of the whole wing. The repair, described in the report of the

Built as B.E.6, 206 was fitted for a time with this experimental undercarriage.

inquiry as so bad '...that it could not possibly be regarded as the work of a conscientious and competent workman', comprised a tapered splice, about seven-and-a-half inches long, so badly made that the glue was up to an eighth of an inch in places. The splice was bound with whipcord in the approved manner, but had not been coated with cobbler's wax as was usual practice, nor had the spar been re-varnished to protect it before the fabric was patched. No record of this repair being carried out could be found and the Committee of Inquiry therefore strongly recommended that all future repairs should be inspected and identity of the workmen and inspector recorded to help prevent similar accidents happening in future. The incident received a fair amount of publicity and the legend of the 'Montrose Ghost' where the restless spirit of Lt Arthur who haunts the airfield has kept the story alive to this day.

B.E.6 was another 'reconstruction', this time a Howard Wright pusher that had previously served with the Air Battalion as F3 before arriving at the Factory for repair. Fitted with an ENV engine, it was originally intended to be reused in the new machine, making it identical to B.E.5 as originally built. However, before it was completed, a second-hand 60-hp Renault became available making the B.E.6 almost identical to B.E.2. The only differences were decking that was fitted at the rear of the engine and a gravity tank that eliminated the teardrop-shaped tank under the upper centre section, a feature of earlier models.

Following its test flight on 5 September, the new machine with the serial 206 was rushed to East Anglia to take part in manoeuvres that were planned to be on a grand scale with some 20,000 troops taking part. It was also planned that twenty aeroplanes would participate, but two fatal accidents involving the structural failure of monoplanes led to a temporary ban on the type until their inherent strengths could be assessed. This left the Royal Flying Corps unable to field the required number of machines and B.E.2, piloted by de Havilland in his capacity as a reserve officer, was one of those brought in to make up the numbers. Thus B.E.1 to B.E.6 all took part and even then only sixteen aeroplanes could be mustered including four from the Naval Wing and Cody's own machine. After the manoeuvres, 206 had a fairly long career serving with 2, 4, 1 and 6 Squadrons. It was fitted for a time with an experimental undercarriage and engaged twice in combat before being struck off charge on 15 September 1915.

Production

Short of aeroplanes and unwilling to wait to see the outcome of the Military Aeroplane competition, the War Office placed orders for three Avro biplanes, four Flanders monoplanes and four examples of the B.E.2. However, the B.E.2s were ordered not from the Royal Aircraft Factory, but from Messrs Vickers Ltd. who were well established as armament contractors with the Factory providing all necessary drawings to ensure that these contractor-built machines would be identical to the original. With the competition over, further orders were placed with a number of contractors for additional examples of the type. Therefore, B.E.2 came

B.E.2, 225, was built by the British & Colonial Aeroplane Company of Bristol. It is seen here on 26 September 1913 after having been flown across the Irish Sea by Lt Dawes. The Elliot instrument panel can be clearly seen in the cockpit.

A B.E.2 assembled and fully rigged but uncovered. This can only have been done for publicity purposes especially as both cockpits are occupied.

to designate a type rather than an individual machine, although only the original ever bore the designation on its rudder.

Production examples were fitted with a 70-hp Renault engine with the taller air scoop and exhausts which ran outside the fuselage, turning down and back to discharge behind and below the rear cockpit. No silencers were fitted, probably because experience had shown that the 'chatter' of the engine's roller bearings, if not louder than the exhaust, could be heard further away.

Early examples had unequal span wings of NPL3a aerofoil section, set at an angle of incidence of four-and-a-half degrees, but these were changed from early 1913 to RAF6. This was developed when it was discovered that the rear spar of the original section had a factor of safety lower than that possible for the main spar and lower than the designers at the Royal Aircraft Factory thought appropriate. The new aerofoil section not only overcame this problem, having spars of equal strength, but when set an angle of incidence of three-and-a-half degrees, gave the same lift with a slight reduction in drag, marginally enhancing performance.

The teardrop-shaped gravity tank, which in early models was suspended below the upper centre section, was eliminated and replaced

An unidentified B.E.2a with wings of unequal span outside the flight shed at Farnborough.

with a tank mounted within decking at the rear of the engine as introduced in the erstwhile B.E.6. The main tank remained under the front seat with a hand pump provided to maintain pressure if necessary. The ignition switch, a simple household type brass-domed light switch, was mounted outside the pilot's cockpit on the port side where it could be clearly seen by the mechanic swinging the propeller. An 'Elliot Bros.' instrument board comprising a column-type air speed indicator rather like a thermometer, a revolutions counter and altimeter was mounted on a board under the decking between the cockpits.

In order to maintain the existence of the fledgling aircraft industry and encourage its growth – or so the War Office believed – small orders were placed with a wide number of contractors including W. G. Armstrong Whitworth and Co., Vickers and the Coventry Ordnance Works. These were better established as armaments contractors than aeroplane manufacturers, although the British & Colonial Aeroplane Company and Handley Page Ltd. also secured orders.

Further Experiments

Modification of the original B.E.2 continued throughout its career. By December 1912, it had been fitted with decking behind the engine as introduced in B.E.6, improving the passenger's comfort. It was, at one point, fitted with a spade-shaped tailplane, increasing its area from thirty-four square feet to fifty-four. Fitting this necessitated shortening the rear fuselage decking by one bay and although, with the experiment concluded, the original, smaller, tailplane was replaced but the shortened decking was retained, becoming a distinguished feature of the machine. Its wheels were covered with fabric to improve streamlining and increase side area, an innovation that was quickly adopted for almost all aeroplanes in service.

At this point, B.E.2 disappears from the Royal Aircraft Factory records as an individual machine, further experiments being conducted on a machine with the serial number 601, the first of a batch of numbers assigned to the Royal Aircraft Factory. From photographic evidence, B.E.2 appears to have suffered an accident on 11 December 1913, but with the Factory's occasionally obscure record keeping, it is unclear whether the original machine was rebuilt or 601 was a new machine.

However, it is possible that the serial number, although assigned earlier, did not appear on the machine until March 1914 when the rudder was replaced by a new component. This was as a result of problems with rudders bending under stress as later described in the following memo distributed by the Royal Aircraft Factory to all units operating the type:

> It has been found with B.E.2 type aeroplanes that when doing extremely sharp turns, or when flying under extreme weather conditions, the rudders become slightly bent. This has never in any way caused any inconvenience to the pilot,

The original B.E.2 after a crash. The photograph is dated 11 December 1913 but no details of the incident have been found. It is fitted with the T3, an experimental tailplane. (*Crown Copyright*)

but it is thought that, by straightening , the rudder could eventually become damaged. Accordingly the rudders and rudder post of all B.E.s are being strengthened.

The problem led to the type being briefly grounded awaiting the new rudders. At a conference on 26 March, it was agreed the type was safe to fly provided that rudders that might have been bent and re-straightened were immediately replaced in case they had been weakened by the process. By June, it had still not been possible to replace the rudders of all B.E.2s in service and pressure was put on all contractors in order to speed up delivery. In March 1914, it was decided to replace a few of the wooden members, which had been formally made from ash, with similar components of spruce. This was done as the quality of ash varies considerably and, although theoretically stronger than spruce in practice, there was often little or no difference in actual compressive strength. Spruce was also lighter. Several squadron commanders complained that the spruce members occasionally appeared to have pockets of 'half dried gum' and expressed concern that they would be weakened by this. Both the Aeronautical Inspection Directorate and the Royal Aircraft Factory responded with assurances that fibres would be continuous around the gum pocket and the components had a factor of safety of between eight and nine, so a little loss of strength could be tolerated. Development of the pneumatic undercarriage that O'Gorman had included in his list of desirable features before B.E.1 was even completed was also undertaken. The first example, modelled on the undercarriage of a contemporary Breguet, was fitted to 206 in October 1912, the machine built as B.E.6 which was in service with 2 Squadron.

This unit was also based at Farnborough so the efficiency of the new undercarriage could be tested under service conditions and yet still be monitored by the Factory. This undercarriage incorporated a single central skid, ending in a spoon-like projection at its forward end. Its work over, it was replaced by a standard twin-skid wooden chassis when the machine was overhauled the following spring.

An oleo undercarriage of a different design, with hook-like steel skids projecting forwards, was fitted for a time and remained in place while the machine was used to conduct other experiments. The final design of

B.E.2 fitted with an experimental undercarriage, one of several designs tested by engineers at the Royal Aircraft Factory.

B.E.2 fitted with experimental fin surfaces above the top wing and with a rectangular tailplane similar to that later adopted for the B.E.2c.

oleo undercarriage – with a central nose wheel serving the same function as the skids fitted to early designs – was also tested on a B.E.2, but found its true home on the larger F.E.2b and the twin-skid unit remained the standard undercarriage for early B.E.2s. This design, in which retained the axle that was bound in place with rubber shock cord to provide an element of springing, was less efficient than the oleo types but far lighter and easy to maintain.

At the end of 1913, crew comfort was improved by the introduction of new fuselage decking with smaller cockpit cut-outs which offered better protection from the elements. This new model, designated B.E.2b, also introduced exposed control cables simplifying inspection and maintenance in the field. No further orders for the B.E.2a were placed and only a limited number of the improved machine were manufactured as something even better was on the way.

O'Gorman, who had expanded the Royal Aircraft Factory to better carry out its research role, frequently recruited graduates from Cambridge University dedicated to such subjects as physics, chemistry and metallurgy. One such student was Edward Teshmaker Busk who had

A production B.E.2b showing alterations to the cockpit sides to give the crew better protection from the elements.

obtained first-class honours in mechanical engineering in 1907, and after a period working in the electrical industry, joined the physics department in June 1912. Busk made a special study of aeroplane stability, carrying out a number of experiments, chiefly with the B.E.2, in order to test his theories. Before he joined the Factory, he had learned to fly at the Aeronautical Syndicate School at Hendon and was able to conduct his own test flights. At the time, stability was considered to be a highly desirable quality for an aeroplane to possess. In an unstable aeroplane, the pilot must, like the rider of a unicycle, be constantly adjusting the balance of his mount, whereas the pilot of a machine that is inherently stable can take his hands off the controls from time to time to do other things. For example, in a military aeroplane, stability would allow the pilot to look around and note troop movements. Lateral stability, as was already known, could be achieved by introducing dihedral by placing the wings at a small angle above the horizontal so as to form a shallow vee. Then, should a gust tip the machine up at one side, the down-going wing would automatically generate lift and so right the machine. Stability in pitch could be achieved by having the tail, not

602 fitted with experimental struts with their upper ends extended to provide fin area as part of E. T. Busk's research into aeroplane stability in October 1913. 602 is surrounded by a crowd of intrigued onlookers as aviation was still very much in its infancy.

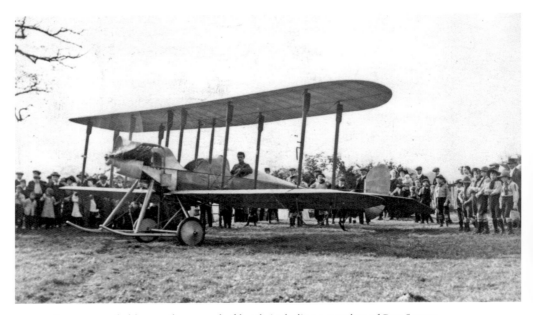

602 surrounded by another crowd of locals including a number of Boy Scouts.

The fin struts and oleo undercarriage fitted together. The pilot's identity is unknown, but it is unlikely to be Busk as he preferred to fly without a leather helmet so he could feel the wind in his hair.

as a lifting surface but as a stabilising one, set at the correct angle to provide a similar righting moment in pitch to that created laterally by dihedral. The elegant tailplane, in whose upper surface O'Gorman had chosen to retain some curvature, i.e. to create lift, was replaced with a plain surface, rectangular in plan and mounted directly on the top longerons, and braced from a kingpost mounted above the rear fuselage. This new stabilising surface was designated T_3 or 'Tailplane No. 3', the large and small curved surfaces previously fitted designated T_1 and T_2 retrospectively. This new tailplane, T_3, provided the righting moment Busk needed to achieve longitudinal stability.

Directional stability was another matter and while Busk knew that the solution lay in having a sufficient vertical surface, he had first to establish how best to arrange it. A vertical tail would provide an answer but was it the best or only answer? He first tried modifying the interplane struts, increasing width at their upper ends so as to provide an additional vertical surface close to the machine's centre of pressure. In another experiment, triangular fins with vertical leading edges were fixed above the centre section struts and the machine flown by Busk to collect data on their effectiveness before deciding that a vertical tail fin was, after all, the best option.

Busk's first stable aeroplane, the R.E.1, elements of which were incorporated in his design for the B.E.2c.

The Royal Aircraft Factory was still a research facility and how many of these experiments were expected to be adopted for use and how many were conducted to see what happened is unclear. But Busk had experimented enough to discover that all he needed to design was a truly stable aeroplane without resorting to the excessive sweepback or similar oddities other designers had thought necessary. His first creation was the R.E.1 (Reconnaissance Experimental No. 1) whose inherent stability caused a sensation, especially when flown 'hands off' before the King and Queen.

He then turned all that he had learned upon the B.E.2 by creating the inherently stable B.E.2c. It was completed at the end of May 1914 by modifying 602, which had then flown for forty-four hours. The fuselage of the new design was similar to that of the B.E.2b, the tailplane replaced with a rectangular surface comparable to the T3, but mounted midway between the upper and lower longerons and wire braced from the rudder post. A triangular fin was added ahead of the rudder. The wings had a redesigned tip profile and were staggered, the lower moving back twenty-four inches with the lower longerons of the forward fuselage modified to provide attachments in the new locations. The wings were still rigged in two bays, but new struts of increased chord were introduced and the

An early B.E.2c showing the staggered wings, triangular fin and rectangular tailplane that distinguished the new model.

wings rigged with three degrees of dihedral. Ailerons were fitted to all four wings, replacing the warping of earlier versions, improving lateral control and allowing the introduction of cross bracing between the interplane struts, thus increasing strength. Later, streamlined wires were introduced that replaced the standard cable, thereby finally completing the list of features O'Gorman had sought to include from the start.

De Havilland's design had been refined into its definitive version, although it was now a very different aeroplane from the one he first flew in December 1911. It was frequently demonstrated by flying 'hands off', sometimes for a considerable time. Pilots were impressed but found flying it so strange after machines that required constant attention to the controls they nicknamed it 'Stability Jane', and later, 'The Quirk'.

Pre-War Service

The first production B.E.2a to enter service was No. 217. Built by British & Colonial, it was accepted following inspection late in January 1913 and joined 2 Squadron on 7 February. The second example, 218, followed soon after. When the squadron moved to Montrose in Scotland in late February, the two B.E.2as were among five machines making the journey north, the others being Maurice Farman pushers. 217 was flown by Captain J. H. W. Becke and 218 by Captain C. A. H. Longcroft. The party set off on 17 February and arrived, after many adventures including

A carefully posed shot of a B.E.2a of 2 Squadron Royal Flying Corps. Since camera shutter speeds at the time could not cope with movement, it is doubtful that the airman would have swung the propeller until the cameraman took his photo. (*Colin Huston*)

Winston Churchill, then First Lord of the Admiralty, poses in front of a B.E.2a. Although he received some instruction, he never qualified as a pilot. However, during the Second World War, he would occasionally wear RAF wings when in uniform.

a change of engine for 217, on 26 February. 218 performed perfectly, the journey seemingly giving Longcroft a taste for long-distance flying. On 21 May, he collected a new B.E.2a, Bristol-built 273, from Farnborough and flew it to Montrose on the same day. Leaving at 5.25 am, Longcroft made two stops for fuel and arrived at 4.20 pm having flown though a hailstorm that battered his face.

Further examples built by a number of contractors arrived for acceptance and were assigned to 2, 4 and 6 Squadrons. A number found their way onto the strength of the Naval Wing and, although the design was greeted with widespread acclaim, here it met a critic. On 31 May 1913, Commander C. R. Samson, who regularly flew No. 46 that had then covered about 1,200 miles, submitted a report on the machine in which he criticised the angle of the bracing wires, lightness of the wing ribs and fit of the interplane struts in their sockets. He also reported that warp wires had worn due in his opinion to the small sizes of the sheaves over which they passed.

O'Gorman responded by stating that the bracing was fine as was the fit of the struts, but declined to comment on the thickness of the ribs which

Adjusting the wireless apparatus fitted to B.E.2a, 220.

had been fully tested. Other squadron commanders, to whom the report had also been sent, replied that wires should be replaced as required and pulleys lubricated as part of routine maintenance. Nonetheless, the two naval machines, 46 and 47, were taken into the Royal Aircraft Factory later that summer and fitted with new wings. Samson appears to have been satisfied by this, and with his confidence restored, later made a personal favourite of another B.E2a, No. 50, one of a pair built by Hewlett & Blondeau. Other units remained generally happy with their B.E.2s, the official history, *The War in the Air*, recorded that:

> Experience ... had favoured the Factory B.E.2. Of the other types most in use the Henri Farman had been found too fatiguing to fly, and the Maurice Farman too slow.

And so the number of B.E.2as in service continued, slowly to increase as the Royal Flying Corps expanded. Two examples, built by British & Colonial, were shipped to Australia for service with the armed forces there.

In 1913, army manoeuvres were held in the Midlands with contingents from 4 and 5 Squadrons on one side and 3 Squadron on the other, although they found it necessary to borrow the newly completed 226 to make up the twelve aircraft required. No. 2 Squadron was not required to attend, instead they flew en masse to Ireland to participate in the manoeuvres

An unidentified B.E.2 during the 1913 manoeuvres. The purpose of the spare wheel in the front cockpit is unknown and may have been needed for another machine.

B.E.2, 206, (the former B.E.6) and 239 on Farnborough Common together with the R.E.1 and at least one Farman. The Royal Aircraft Factory buildings are in the background.

held there. B.E.2s number 217, 218, 225, 272 and 273 were amongst those that made the crossing over the Irish Sea from Stranraer to Larne, for which they were fitted with flotation bags. These, in the universal opinion of the pilots who flew them, made the machines sluggish in taking-off and difficult to handle if the weather was rough. Fortunately,

B.E.2s of 2 Squadron fitted with flotation bags to cross the Irish Sea and take part in manoeuvres in Ireland.

their efficiency at keeping the machine afloat if it was forced down in the sea was never tested in practice. During the event, the machines each flew about 1,000 miles in addition to the return journey from Scotland.

Longcroft, his appetite for long-distance flying unsatisfied, had in August flown a B.E.2a, 225, from the depot at Farnborough to Montrose carrying Major F. H. Sykes as a passenger with just one stop at Alnmouth to refuel. Then, on 22 November, he took his long-distance flying to the limit. 218 was fitted with a special petrol tank made on the squadron's premises by Air Mechanic H. C. S. Bullock, the tank located in the front cockpit and faired over with fabric. With an additional fifty-three gallons of petrol onboard, roughly twice the weight of a passenger, Longcroft took-off from Montrose. He flew south until he reached the south coast at Portsmouth where he turned around and returned to Farnborough covering 550 miles nonstop in seven hours and twenty minutes. For this feat he was awarded the Royal Aero Club's Britannia Trophy for the most meritorious of the year.

Throughout June 1914, almost the entire Royal Flying Corps gathered at Netheravon for a 'concentration camp' at which the various squadrons could jointly undertake training and participate in exercises together. No. 2 Squadron flew its ten B.E.2as down from Montrose in short stages designed to allow its motor transport to keep pace.

218 after modification for long-distance flying with the front cockpit faired over to house additional fuel tanks. Capt. Longcroft is in the cockpit.

331 with the Royal Aircraft Factory's balloon shed and airship hangar in the background. Serving with 2 Squadron, it crashed on 15 May 1914 near Northallerton while en route from Montrose to Netheravon killing the crew, Lt Empson and A/M Cudmore.

229 at Horsham with the expected crowd of spectators in 1914.

The exercise was in many ways a dress rehearsal for mobilisation in preparation for war and the crews knew it. Training was key and almost every day there were lectures and exercises of one kind or another all intended to improve the efficiency of the Royal Flying Corps. On one particular day, there were as many as thirty aeroplanes in the air to the amazement of the residents of nearby Salisbury. On another day, Lts Swain and James flew two B.E.2s, each equipped with a wireless set, from Netheravon down to the south coast at Bournemouth, passing messages back and forth en route.

On 9 June, Major W. S. Brancker, officer in charge of Royal Flying Corps supplies, flew from Farnborough in the prototype B.E.2c. After take-off, Brancker climbed to 2,000 feet, set course for Salisbury Plain and was then flown 'hands off' for the duration of the journey with slight adjustments of the rudder to maintain course. Brancker, who was almost proud of his indifferent skills as a pilot, was duly impressed and passed the time writing a reconnaissance report on the countryside over which he flew. The purpose of his visit and reason for making it in 602 is unrecorded, but whatever it was for, it was brief as Brancker returned to Farnborough the same afternoon.

Major Burke was evidently absent when the B.E.2c made its brief visit to Netheravon but heard all about it from his crews and, on 16 June, sent the following request to Royal Flying Corps headquarters:

I understand that it is possible to convert the existing B.E.2's into the type of machine which is inherently stable and which, I believe, is to be called B.E.2c. As we are returning to Montrose at the beginning of next month, I should be very glad if I could do so, with some men thoroughly trained on the new machine. I would therefore be glad if you could consider whether I might convert an existing B.E. of my Squadron into a B.E.2c while we are here.

The request was supported by Burke's superior, Lt Col F. H. Sykes, and forwarded to the Director General of Military Aeronautics who left it to O'Gorman to explain that a conversion was possible. However, the resulting machine would not be a B.E.2c and that the matter was being discussed at the War Office, but that the wide-scale adoption of the new type seemed likely. Although Burke requested to be issued a B.E.2c before his return north, none were available and had to make do with a promise to issue the type as soon as possible. Probably as a result of this exchange of correspondence, B.E.2c 602, returned to Netheravon on 19 June, again flown by Brancker, remaining there until 26 June to give service pilots an opportunity to familiarise themselves with the new machine. On the return journey to Farnborough it was piloted be Lt Sheppard (Royal Navy).

347 was long thought to have been the first British aeroplane to land in France, but was damaged on 6 August 1914 and finished its career at the Central Flying School. It is seen here near Scarborough in June 1914 with its pilot, Lt Harvey-Kelly, seated against a haystack smoking a cigarette.

On 1 July, Burke closed the exchange with the following report:

> With reference to the new type of machine which has been called B.E.2c, I
> have to report that this machine was flown by all the experienced pilots of
> my Squadron. The result of the trial was to show that, as far as we could
> see, the machine is inherently more stable than any other type, and in other
> respects presented no peculiar features. I was informed of several ideas as to
> peculiarities but they were not borne out by our experience.

602 was to spend time with 3 Squadron in July and 4 Squadron in
August so that the crews could gain valuable experience with it before
being returned to the Aircraft Park. Meanwhile, the Royal Flying Corps
would have to soldier on with their existing B.E.2as. The B.E.2b would
only begin to enter service in August and production of the B.E.2c would
not follow until the next year.

Further Testing

Testing of the B.E.2 continued even after it had entered production not only to check that it was safe for the duties it was required to carry out, but to verify the stress calculations made by the Farnborough team so that future designs could be made with increased confidence. Therefore, a rig was produced in which a wing could be warped to several degrees while carrying twice its normal load. 350,000 movements were made without damage to the wing. Every single component was tested beyond its normal load capacity and proved adequate. This process, and the results obtained, was made public in May 1914 by the publication of the report entitled 'Precautions Taken as to the Strength of the B.E. class Aeroplane' so that designers in the industry might have the benefit of the Royal Aircraft Factory's research.

On 14 March 1914, the War Office informed Col F. H. Sykes, Officer Commanding the Royal Flying Corps (Military Wing) that whichever B.E.2 currently in service had reached 100 hours flying time should be handed over to the Aeronautical Inspection Department for testing. Sykes selected 226, a Bristol-built machine then with 2 Squadron at Montrose. 226 was therefore flown to Farnborough arriving on 7 April and at handover had flown ninety-nine hours and six minutes. It was inspected by none other than Geoffrey de Havilland, then inspector of aeroplanes with the Aeronautical Inspection Department (AID), the body responsible for quality control. De Havilland reported that although some bolt holes had worn slightly oval and a few cables showed signs of fraying where they passed over pulleys, the machine was generally in good condition and had been well maintained despite having spent twenty-nine nights in the open unprotected from the elements.

On 23 April, in the presence of a number of Royal Flying Corps personnel, Factory staff and officials, the B.E.2 was inverted and the

226 made a close attempt to beat the altitude record and, after 100 hours flying, was tested to destruction to prove that design factors of safety were being met.

wings loaded, first with bags of lead shot then with loose sand while tension in the rigging wires was monitored. At a load of 9,600 lbs, the cross member carrying the front bearing of the warp mechanism shaft cracked but remained intact. Thereafter, the warp was exercised from time to time to check that it still functioned and loading continued until a total load of 11,725 lbs was evenly applied. Suddenly, the port side wing assembly collapsed. At this point, the load in the wing spars, which remained undamaged, exceeded 5.7 proving that the design factor of safety of six had been achieved.

As a result of this test it was accepted that both the design strength and standards of maintenance within the Royal Flying Corps were satisfactory and no changes to either were therefore advised.

Aware that Renault had its faults, and anxious to provide the B.E.2 with more power, the Royal Aircraft factory embarked upon the design of a new engine of their own, designated with compelling logic, the RAF1. This was an 8.8-litre V8, based on the Renault. In order to allow each big end to have a separate crank journal, the cylinders were slightly offset, those on the right being slightly ahead of those on the left. The crankshaft was a hollow forging supported in roller bearings which gave the engine its characteristic chatter when running. Cylinder heads were cast integral with the finned iron cylinders, eliminating any potential problems with a gasket joint and were held down with four long bolts. The pistons were of cast iron with slightly domed heads, each having four grooves, three

A B.E.2 wing loaded with bags of shot and then loose sand as a test of strength. (*Crown Copyright*)

of which were fitted with rings and the fourth left empty to carry oil. A single camshaft operated overhead exhaust valves by pushrods and rockers, and the inlet side valves directly, via tappets, the valves having removable seats to facilitate maintenance. As in the Renault, the propeller ran on the camshaft drive, thus rotating at half-engine speed, the spur gear drive strengthened to carry the load. A specially-made Claudel-Hobson carburettor was fitted and comprised two barrels, one for each cylinder bank, sharing a single float chamber. A lightweight internal flywheel acted as an oil pump, delivering oil into a passage cast in the end cover from where it ran in channels to the bearings. Breather pipes, reminiscent of ship ventilators, then discharged an oil mist onto the exposed valve gear and surrounding areas. Oil consumption was around five pints per hour and it was usual to fill the sump with twenty-five pints before a flight, although thirty was recommended if the flight was expected to be of unusually long duration. Twin magnetos were fitted, one for each cylinder bank, the timing fixed and set to fire when the piston was 12 mm before the top of its stroke. Later, an eight-cylinder magneto was developed, simplifying the engine and slightly reducing its weight. The first example was bench tested late in April 1914 and delivered a steady 78 hp, measured on a brake, and consumed fifty-and-a-half imperial gallons of petrol during the eight-hour test. Development would bring its output, at its normal speed of 1,600 rev/min, up to around 90 hp, and at this power output the type was rated when put into production as the RAF1a.

The burnt-out remains of 601 after the accident that caused the untimely death of E. T. Busk, designer of the stable B.E.2c.

On 5 November, Busk took-off in 601 at 4.35 pm and climbed above Farnborough Common. However, at 800 feet, a light was seen in the cockpit and the machine caught fire where it glided to the ground where both the B.E.2c and pilot were consumed by the flames. One theory to explain the cause of the fire is that petrol leaked onto the hot exhaust. Factory staff believed that Busk was carrying a pyrotechnic device that ignited prematurely, which would account for his taking-off after the sun had set. Whether this was an experimental weapon or a prank is unclear, but whatever the cause, the result was the same. Not only was Ted Busk dead, but the Factory's sole B.E.2c and prototype RAF1 engine were destroyed.

Mr Clive Wigram, the King's Equerry, who had flown with Busk in R.E.1, sent a letter of condolence on behalf of the King and Queen who remembered him from their visit to Farnborough the previous May. Busk was buried with full honours as befitted his rank as a lieutenant in the Territorial Army in Aldershot Military Cemetery.

With 601 wrecked and 602 in France, it was not until January 1915 when production examples became available. The Central Flying School finally got its chance to evaluate the B.E.2c and on 23 January published this report on B.E.2c, 1751:

Gliding

The machine glides steadily at about 50mph and with passenger at 55mph. The machine, if left entirely alone, engine shut off, takes up her normal gliding angle, but it is necessary in order to land her properly to use the elevator just before reaching the ground. She would probably land herself, but somewhat heavily.

Climbing

With or without passenger, if left alone, she climbs steadily at about 55mph. Rate of climb is somewhat slow but steady. When climbing in the usual way by using the controls, she climbs about 3,000 feet (full load) on an average, in 10 minutes.

Lateral Control

The machine banks unaided according to the amount of rudder used. On very steep turns the nose requires holding up to prevent a somewhat excessive increase of speed. This also applies to a steep spiral descent with engine off. All normal and reasonable turns require no assistance with the elevator.

Bad Weather

The machine requires no assistance at all in winds of up to 30mph, although a little assistance is more comfortable. When assistance is given she is equally controllable by warp (sic) or rudder.

Landing

A little sluggish in coming off the glide – probably owing to the large tailplane damping any violent movement.

Longitudinal Stability

The engine was shut off, a short dive made, the lever pulled back; she reared up to a moderate angle, lost flying speed, dived and repeated the performance three times, the cloche being permanently held back. There was no sign of side slip and the dives and rears were gradually damping out. Under all conditions of stalling it would seem the machine would be quite safe above 50-75 feet from the ground.

General Opinion

With the 70 hp Renault she is, I think, a fraction under-powered. The rudder bar might, with advantage, be fitted with straps. Thus with one leg disabled, and the lateral and fore & aft controls destroyed, she would still be under control with engine or rudder, or for a glide without engine.

Off to War

When the Royal Flying Corps mobilised for war it was able to field just four complete squadrons: Nos 2, 3, 4 and 5. No. 1 was still in the process of converting from airships and No. 6, although formed some months earlier, was incomplete. Of these, both No. 2 and No. 4 were fully equipped with the B.E.2, No. 3 flew a mixture of Bleriot monoplanes and Henri Farman pushers while No. 4 had Avros, Farmans and a flight of B.E.8s. The Aircraft Park, which supplied replacement machines to the squadrons, had three Farmans, four Sopwiths, nine B.E.2as and the prototype B.E.2c in stock. Therefore, not only was the B.E.2 the

A French postcard depicting the arrival of B.E.2a, 318, in France with 4 Squadron on 13 August 1914. Built by the Coventry Ordnance Works, it had a fairly short war career being struck off charge on 13 October.

228 served with 2 Squadron before the war and went to France on 13 August 1914. It was condemned shortly after arrival as unfit for further service.

most numerous single type, it represented more than half the Royal Flying Corp's effective strength. No. 6, when it too arrived in France, was equipped with eight B.E.2as and four Henri Farmans, increasing the ratio further. That not one of these aeroplanes was armed was not considered in any way remarkable.

The first four squadrons flew to France on 13 August, the first aeroplane to land being B.E.2a, 327, of 2 Squadron, piloted by Capt. F. Waldron. A few days later, a Bleriot of 3 Squadron piloted by Lt Joubert de la Ferte and 4 Squadron's Lt G. W. Mapplebecke in a B.E.2, carried out the Royal Flying Corp's first reconnaissance mission of the war.

B.E.2c, 602, was crated and shipped for its trip to France and confusion arose as to its identity, therefore when assembled it was renumbered 807. On 2 September, the B.E.2c was issued to 2 Squadron therefore fulfilling the promise made to Major Burke. However, it was later discovered that this serial number had been allocated to another machine. In October, the B.E.2c was renumbered once more, this time as 1807. New squadrons arrived in France as soon as they could be formed, many of them equipped with the B.E.2, the stable platform best suited to the needs of time. The Bleriots, Farmans and other miscellaneous designs with which the pre-war Royal Flying Corps had been equipped

Above left: B.E.2b, 650, of 2 Squadron Royal Flying Corps after a bad landing showing the Union Jack marking adopted early in the war. They were changed to the familiar roundel when it was realised the flag could be mistaken for the German cross at a distance.

Above right: Another view of 650. Markings were applied only to the underside to aid identification from the ground. As yet, an attack from above was not considered a serious threat.

were phased out and relegated to a training role, leaving the B.E.2 as the only pre-war design in large scale service. Production of the B.E.2c was increased with orders placed for batches of twenty or more at a time and new manufacturers were added to the lists of those building the aeroplane to cope with increasing demand.

At first it was a war of movement for which the Royal Flying Corps had been trained, mainly reconnaissance searching the countryside for enemy troops and reporting their position. But as the trench lines formed and the war changed to that of bloody attrition, the role of the aircraft also transformed. The new reconnaissance role involved studying areas behind the German lines for evidence of increased activity that might

Above: B.E.2c, 1744, of 12 Squadron Royal Flying Corps was shot down by anti-aircraft fire behind enemy lines on 26 September 1915.

Right: Another view of 1744 showing the combination of markings, roundels on the fuselage and small Union Jacks under the wings.

indicate a forthcoming attack. Also, artillery observation became more important, reporting the fall of shot as the big guns sought to destroy the enemy's own artillery, stores and soldiers.

Bombing was a new task for the B.E.2c. Although bombsights were nonexistent and the bombs puny, the crews used enthusiasm and ingenuity to make up for what they lacked in equipment.

On 26 May 1915, 2nd Lt William Rhodes-Moorhouse was sent in B.E.2b, 687, to bomb the railway at Courtrai, hoping to disable the

Above: B.E.2b, 487, of 4 Squadron was forced to land behind enemy lines during a bombing raid on Lille on 11 March 1915 and was evaluated in Germany. (*Imperial War Museum*)

Left: 2nd Lt William Rhodes-Moorhouse whose courageous bombing raid earned him the Victoria Cross. (*Colin Huston*)

tracks that would slow the flow of reinforcements reaching the Battle of Neuve Chapelle. Flying solo, Rhodes-Moorhouse dropped his 112 lbs bomb at 300 feet as to ensure accuracy and managed to hit and damage the tracks. However, at such a low height, he was subjected to a barrage of small arms fire and was shot in the stomach, hand and thigh. Rather than landing to seek medical attention, Rhodes-Moorhouse returned to his squadron at Estaires to report his success and prevent another pilot being sent to repeat the attack. Although rushed to a field hospital, he died of his wounds the following day and was awarded a posthumous Victoria Cross for his courageous self-sacrifice.

Development Continues

Following the loss of the prototype B.E.2c, 601, the Royal Aircraft Factory adopted an early production example, 1749, which was built by Vickers and completed just before the end of 1914 as a test vehicle for its continued development of the design. By 7 January 1915, it was fitted with a new and simplified undercarriage of the type that was to become the norm for almost all aeroplanes throughout the next decade. This comprised two inverted wooden vees with an axle fixed within their apexes and bound in place with thirty-eight feet of 3/8 rubber shock cord.

B.E.2c, 1749, that replaced 601 as the Royal Aircraft Factory's test vehicle.

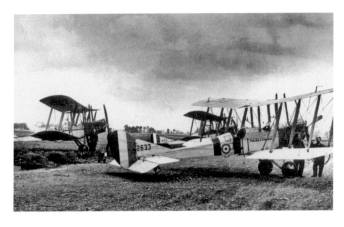

B.E.2cs of
16 Squadron in
France, 1915.

The next improvement was the installation of a 90-hp RAF1a engine in place of the Renault with which the machine had been built. New exhausts were fitted which discharged above the centre section to prevent exhaust gases finding their way into the cockpits, and the sump was enclosed in a neat cowling, improving both its appearance and streamlining. The cable bracing was replaced with more streamlined 'Rafwires' which were swaged to a lenticular section and threaded at the ends to allow adjustment. The pilot was now provided with an instrument panel to which were fitted a dial-type air speed indicator, altimeter, revolutions counter, compass, clinometer and a watch, the latter detachable and a highly-prized souvenir.

These improvements not only changed the appearance of the machine but so affected its flying characteristics. In May 1915, when the first B.E.2c powered by the RAF1a arrived in France, a brief document was prepared and printed by Harrison & Sons on behalf of Her Majesty's Stationary Office (HMSO) for distribution to the pilots in all squadrons operating the B.E.2. It read:

> A Note for Flyers of B.E.2c Aeroplanes fitted with RAF1a Engines, V type Undercarriages and Rafwires.
>
> 1) ADJUSTMENT; The aeroplane should be so adjusted so that it is in trim when flying at "cruising" speed – from 65 to 70 miles per hour. At this speed the machine will then fly without the controls.
>
> 2) REVOLUTIONS ON THE GROUND; On the ground, the engine revolutions should be between 1,480 and 1,520 per min.; but under

no circumstance should this, or any other engine, be allowed to run at full throttle until after it has warmed up, and the oil is circulating freely throughout the engine. This will require at least 10 minutes slow running.

3) CLIMBING SPEEDS; With full tanks and passenger, the best climbing speed is about 55 miles per hour, and the engine revolutions at this speed should be 1,600 per min. During a test made by the Aeronautical Inspection Department, a climb of 6,000 ft in 13 mins 35 secs, may be obtained; and on service at least 6,000 ft in 16 mins may be expected.

4) MAXIMUM SPEED; At the maximum speed of the aeroplane, when flying at a low altitude, the engine revolutions will approximate to 1,850 ft per min; but at this speed, the fuel consumption will reach 9 gallons of petrol per hour, and if the maximum time in the air is desired the normal engine revolutions of 1,600 per min should be maintained.

5) LANDING SPEED; The landing speed is much the same as with the Renault engined B.E.2c – about 40 to 41 miles per hour, but there is a strong tendency for flyers to alight at too high a speed until they become accustomed to flying this machine, owing to its higher normal speed, 80.6 miles per hour on an Aeronautical Inspection Department test, or 87 miles per hour under service conditions. It should be noted that the gliding angle of this machine is finer than that of the old B.E.'s.

6) FUEL CONSUMPTION; the petrol consumption at the normal engine speed of 1,600 revs per min is 7¼ gallons per hour; but this will vary with the elevation at which the flight is made, being somewhat reduced as height is increased.

The leaflet then continued with a four-page description of the construction, operation and maintenance of the engine, and concluded with the following advice on flying the machine, reinforcing the advice previously given:

Open throttle full, and the motor should run 1,800 revs per min when climbing. When sufficient height has been reached, throttle the motor so that the revolutions are about 1,600. This is the intended normal speed of the motor and, flying level at 1,600 revs per min, the consumption of petrol will not exceed 7½ gallons an hour and will probably be 6½ gallons. If extra speed is required the motor may be accelerated to 1,800 revs per min, but the petrol will be increased to 9 gallons per hour, or a little more if flying low.

The B.E.2c crews, with the fatalistic humour that characterised the First World War, composed their own note on their mounts in the form of the following poem:

The Pilot's Psalm
The B.E.2c is my bus, therefore I shall want.
He maketh me to come down in green pastures,
He leadeth me where I will not go.
He maketh me to be sick, he leadeth me astray on all cross-country flights.
Yea, though I fly over no-man's land where mine enemies would encompass me about I fear much evil, for thou art with me.
Thy joystick and thy prop discomfort me,
Thou prepares a crash for me in the presence of mine enemies,
Thy RAF anointed me with oil,
Thy tank leaked badly,
Surely to goodness thou shalt not follow me all the days of my life
Or I shall dwell in the House of Colney Hatch forever.

In early 1915, Mr Samuel Hiscocks, the Royal Aircraft Factory's assistant superintendent, had made a trip to France, visiting squadrons operating Factory-designed machines and reported as follows:

Nos. 2 and 6 Squadrons mentioned that the B.E.2c with the 70 hp Renault when getting away from the ground or just alighting in a strong cross wind tended to turn down wind. This is more noticeable with the B.E.2c than with the B.E.2a and B.E.2b machines owing to the smaller reserve of power. With the B.E.2c's having the RAF1 engine this tendency should not be so noticeable, as the reserve of power will be increased nearly 100 per cent.

Immediately upon Hiscocks' return to Farnborough, an investigation was made by the Factory's chief test pilot, Frank Goodden. No Renault-powered machine was available and Goodden carried out the test in a B.E.2c powered by an RAF1a, presumably 1749. He took-off in a southerly direction, at right angles to a strong wind blowing from the west, and during the take-off run the machine was blown to the east. After take-off, Goodden turned into the wind and at 500 feet found that the machine virtually stood still when flying at its lowest speed and therefore concluded that the wind speed, at that height, was about 35-

40 mph. Goodden reported that a very long run had been necessary to take-off safely and that, in a machine more heavily loaded or powered by the Renault engine instead of the RAF1a, it would have been quite dangerous. Goodden found no tendency to turn away from the wind, but rather the reverse, the machine on the ground showing tendency to turn into wind that he had had to correct with the rudder. On 7 May, O'Gorman forwarded this report to the War Office together with praise for Goodden's bravery in carrying out the trials. He also added that the difficulty arose from the choice of bad flying grounds and that, with properly chosen airfields, the necessity for taking-off crosswind should not arise. O'Gorman further suggested that the following advice be issued to pilots:

> Getting Off in a Side Wind.
> Pilots should remember that for getting off in a side wind a very much longer run is necessary. The following is the method of procedure recommended;-
> (1). When starting rudder hard to prevent aeroplane turning into wind.
> (2). As the aeroplane gathers speed ease off rudder. Keep the aeroplane straight.
> (3). As the aeroplane gets off bank gently and turn into the wind as soon as possible.

While this advice to pilots helped them to operate the B.E.2c, engineers at the Royal Aircraft Factory were aware that the type was capable of improvement, especially in top speed and rate of climb. Both could be improved by an increase in engine power and so attempts were made to get more out of the RAF1. A new version, its compression ratio increased, was developed and bench tested at an output of 105 hp at 1,800 rev/min; however, cooling and reliability were both adversely affected by the modification and it did not go into production. Another version, the RAF1b – in which the bore was increased from 100 to 105 mm, increasing its displacement to 9.7 litres – gave a similar increase in power, but cooling, which was marginal in the standard engine, was again an issue. A supercharged version was also developed and when fitted to a B.E.2c, its climb was improved from 8,500 in thirty-six minutes to 11,500 feet in a similar time. Despite this improvement, it was not adopted for mass production, largely due to the inevitable delay to output that it would cause.

Frank Goodden, the Royal Aircraft Factory's chief test pilot looping a B.E.2c over Farnborough Common.

If the 90-hp engine were to be retained, as seemed most likely, solutions to the improvements in speed and climb initially appeared mutually exclusive. The top speed could be increased by reducing the area of the wings, but this would adversely affect the rate of climb and result in an increase in landing speed. While climb could be improved by an increase in wing area, this would create additional drag and reduce the maximum speed. The answer was a more efficient wing, one that would increase lift and yet reduce drag. The Factory had, in conjunction with the National Physical Laboratory, been experimenting with new wing sections for some time but none had proved superior to that already in use, i.e. a section based on RAF6 but with an increased under camber.

In the summer of 1915, a breakthrough was made with RAF14 that offered a distinct improvement with an increase in lift and a reduction in drag. Tests were moved out of the laboratory for full-scale trials with the new section given to the workshops on 19 August 1915. It was necessary to modify the section slightly to simplify manufacture, which delayed completion, but the change fortunately had little adverse effect on performance.

A B.E.2c fitted with the robust oleo undercarriage that found a more appropriate home on the F.E.2b.

Fitted with wings of the new section, the top speed of the B.E.2c increased by 4 mph, and although not a significant increase, was useful and would have required an additional 14 hp to achieve with the previous wing section. Climb was less easy to assess, an accurate measurement requiring numerous tests in differing weathers, but a simple climb to 6,000 feet in a machine fitted with the original wings took fifteen minutes; a similarly powered B.E.2c fitted with the new wings took just fourteen minutes to reach the same height. Tests flights were undertaken by two Royal Aircraft Factory pilots, Frank Goodden and William Stutt, and neither could detect any difference in either landing or stalling speeds. These improvements in performance could be obtained by the simple expedient of issuing new drawings and wings of RAF14 section were therefore substituted for all B.E.2s from that point on.

Meanwhile, 1749's career as a test vehicle continued, and in June 1915, was fitted with an improved Rouzet wireless set, development of which was one of the many areas of aeroplane design investigated by the Royal Aircraft Factory's scientists. Wireless development was later conducted by a separate unit within the Royal Flying Corps based in Hounslow and then relocated to Biggin Hill in Kent where the airfield's hilltop location improved the range obtained. The robust oleo undercarriage adopted for the big pusher F.E.2b was also experimentally fitted to a B.E.2c, but reduced performance without offering any significant improvement in landing.

Bristol-built 1688 was another machine adopted by the Royal Aircraft Factory as a test vehicle. By June 1915, it had been fitted with an oleo undercarriage and later with a larger, balanced rudder. Its upper centre section was, at one time, covered with transparent cellon dope in an attempt to improve the pilot's upward view. In December 1915, it was used to test the Factory's new low-level bombsight developed by R. H. Mayo and was later used to test the Fiery Grapnel, a device invented for use against Zeppelins. This device comprised a pair of hooks fitted on the end of a cable and towed behind the aeroplane with the intention of attaching itself to the enemy airship whereupon the cable would break and the device explode, igniting escaping hydrogen gas. Like many weird ideas for weaponry, it was not adopted.

Another experiment intended as defence against Zeppelins was the Airship Plane in which a B.E.2c was suspended beneath an SS-class non-rigid airship envelope, replacing the car. The idea being that the ensemble

The ingenious but unsuccessful Fiery Grapnel installed on a B.E.2c.

The first Airship Plane at Kingsnorth. The airship's controls were later modified to include additional surfaces in order to improve control but no planned release was made.

could stay aloft until a raiding Zeppelin was sighted whereupon the crew would release the envelope and fly off to attack. Initial trials were made at Kingsnorth in August 1915, the device piloted by Flt Cmdr W. C. Hicks, but control problems meant that no release was made and the Airship Plane landed intact. A further trial was made on 21 February 1916 using B.E.2c, 989, and with the idea's instigators, Cmdr N. F. Unwin and Sqn Cmdr deC. W. P. Ireland, in the cockpits. However, at about 4,000 feet, a sudden loss of pressure in the envelope caused the forward suspension wires to release the nose of the B.E.2c that dropped down breaking the remaining wires. As it fell, the aeroplane's controls were damaged and the B.E.2c dived in a sideslip. During the violent manoeuvre, Ireland was thrown out and fell into the River Medway and drowned, the doomed B.E.2c crashing near Strood railway station, killing Unwin. The experiment was promptly discontinued, and although a revised proposal using a manned rigid airship was eventually successful, the B.E.2c had no further involvement.

In an attempt to steepen the B.E.2c's angle of glide and so facilitate landing in small, constricted fields, the Factory's physics department devised an early form of airbrake. The struts could be turned at right angles, so presenting their broad face to the airflow and therefore creating additional drag. B.E.2c, 4550, a production machine built by G & J. Weir, was modified in December 1915 and the idea tested with the trials concluding on 9 January 1916. The results, as described in 'H' Department's Report No. 917, were that an additional resistance of 61 lbs at 100 feet per second was achieved that steepened the glide angle at 60 mph from 1 in 6.5 without the brakes, to 1 in 5.6 with them operated. This improvement was not considered sufficient to justify the complication of the mechanism required to achieve it and the idea was scrapped. The same aeroplane was employed to test the action of gyroscopes in a series of experiments in connection with the development of an automatic pilot, but the device, although offering very promising results, was not sufficiently developed for adoption at the time. Another production machine, 4721, which had seen service with 24 Squadron and at the School of Aerial Gunnery, was, towards the end of 1916, fitted with floats manufactured by the well-known boat builders S. E. Saunders of Cowes and successfully test flown from Loch Doon. The main float was a single box-like structure and was attached to the skid of the machine's early pattern undercarriage in what appears to have been a repetition of an experiment first carried out in 1912. More sophisticated floats had been developed and the reason for the trial has not been discovered.

Mass Production

The first production B.E.2c completed was 1748, built by Vickers, which was presented for final inspection by the Aeronautical Inspection Department on 19 December 1914. A presentation machine – that is one paid for either by subscription or donation – it proudly bore the name of its sponsor *Liverpool* in large letters along the fuselage sides. Later presentation aircraft would have such information in a more discreet panel, close to the nose, where it did not interfere with military markings.

1695, a Renault-powered B.E.2c built by The British & Colonial Aeroplane Company. At first, presentation machines had the donor's name boldly painted on the fuselage as seen here, but later a more discreet style was adopted.

The first B.E.2c built by Sir William Beardmore & Co. Ltd. at the company's works. The naval officer may have been the pilot.

The British & Colonial Aeroplane Company's first B.E.2c, 1652, was completed two weeks later and was inspected on 4 January 1915, while the first from Sir W. G. Armstrong, Whitworth & Co., was not ready until 2 February.

1652 was the first production example to reach France, entering service with 2 Squadron on 13 February. Thereafter, deliveries continued at a slow pace and by 1 April, just twelve were in service: four each with No. 2, 6 and 16 Squadrons, the earlier B.E.2as and B.E.2bs continuing to fly on operations and to give good service. Although efforts were made to expand the Royal Flying Corps and Royal Navy Air Service, progress was hampered both by the need to train pilots and the limited capacity of aircraft manufacturing. Therefore, by the end of 1915, there were only 120 B.E.2cs in services spread over nineteen squadrons. The first production machines were built by pre-war aeroplane manufacturers such as British & Colonial, Handley Page Ltd., and Grahame-White, or by aviation departments of established armaments contractors like Vickers Ltd., Armstrong, Whitworth and the Coventry Ordnance Works. Nonetheless, it was soon clear that the manufacturing capacity would have to be severely expanded if the needs of the growing air services were to be met.

Aeroplane design is a very specialised field, requiring both a natural flair and a great deal of scientific knowledge, but the manufacture of

5384, first of a batch of Renault-engined B.E.2cs built by Wolseley Motors with a group of workmen on the left. They had every reason to be proud of the superbly finished machine.

A head-on view of 5384 taken on the same occasion.

aeroplanes was a different matter. The construction of an aeroplane of this period, although complex and based on sound engineering principals, in essence comprised a considerable number of relatively simple components assembled together to form the whole. For example, there is no fundamental difference in the making of, say, an undercarriage or wing strut to the making of a wheel spoke or banister post. A wing spar or a longeron are simply pieces of planed wood, routed out for lightness, and any woodworking shop could make them. Similarly, a fabricated metal fitting is much like another and the tradesman who can make one can easily make another: all he needs is a drawing to work from. And it was here that the Royal Aircraft Factory design truly came into its own. Unlike other private aircraft companies where it was not unusual to draw a proposed aeroplane full size in chalk as a working template, the Farnborough drawing office had produced detailed drawings for every component. These could be easily reproduced and issued to contractors seeking to take up aircraft manufacture.

More than twenty companies from a wide range of backgrounds accepted orders to build the B.E.2. Of these, Frederick Sage & Co. were shop fitters who had been responsible for the interior of Harrods department store; both Barclay Curle and Napier & Miller were shipbuilders, as were William Denny; G. & J. Weir of Glasgow were manufacturers of specialist pumping equipment; Daimler were well known manufacturers of high-class motor cars; and Ruston & Procter built steam engines. Two things that all these companies, diverse as their business interests were, had in common were available workshop space and a desire to aid the war effort. Some skills, such as fabric covering, had to be learned from scratch and it was found that in this field as in oxy-acetylene welding, women were more skilled than men.

The Daimler company, like Wolseley Motors, were manufacturers of motor cars and also undertook aircraft manufacturing and built the RAF1a engine. The first production example, from Daimler, Number 21955/WD271, was completed in March 1915. Fitted to Bristol-built B.E.2c, 1687, it went to France on 11 May and served with 2 Squadron. Daimler had won the contract to build the engines in a competitive tender before the outbreak of the war and carried out some development of the design to aid production. When other manufacturers were needed to boost output, Daimler generously assisted their rivals in setting up production.

4452 under construction in the works of J. & G. Weir.

B.E.2gs being built at the Daimler works. The aeroplane nearest to the camera is A3113.

B728 was a rebuild produced by the Southern Aeroplane Repair Depot at Farnborough.

Later in the war, the B.E.2c and other aircraft were created at the Southern Aeroplane Repair Depot. Based in Farnborough, reclaimed components were refurbished, repaired as necessary, and assembled into new machines.

A Rival Machine

One of the contractors building the early model B.E.2c was Sir Armstrong, Whitworth & Co, Ltd. of Newcastle whose chief designer, Frederick Koolhoven, studied the machine and thought that he could do better, simplifying the design to improve performance and make manufacture simpler. His proposal was to replace the twin skid undercarriage with a central skid and oleo pneumatic shock absorbers, similar to experimental models tried at Farnborough. Also, the swivelling tailskid with a fixed skid was replaced by a fitted leaf spring. Koolhoven designed new wings with raked tips, still braced in two bays, but with some of the original wires eliminated. The tailplane was repositioned to sit on the upper longerons, as it had done in the original B.E.2, the fin and rudder being retained. The fuselage decking was modified, leaving the crew positions unaltered, and the engine exhaust joined to form a single vertical discharge pipe on the machine's centreline ahead of the forward cockpit. The Armstrong Experimental Machine as it was then known was examined in February 1915 – and possibly due to their established reputation as an armament manufacturer rather than any significant merit in the design – a contract, No 94/A/103, was placed for a total of seven prototypes, serial 5328 to 5334, which the manufacturers designated FK2 to be built for evaluation.

One of these, 5332, was tested in France by Norman Spratt, a former Royal Aircraft Factory test pilot who considered it no better than the B.E.2c. He was highly critical of the lateral control and thought that it might prove dangerous to fly in bad weather. Gen. Trenchard, commander of the Royal Flying Corps in France, thought that its twenty-eight gallon petrol tank was too small, and not wishing to have the complication of maintaining stocks of spares for two rival designs, recommended that it was not adopted.

The Armstrong Whitworth FK2 was an attempt to improve on the B.E.2 design to facilitate manufacture and developed into the FK3 as seen here at the company's works at Gosforth.

However, Armstrong Whitworth's reputation carried the day for orders had been placed and hundreds of a modified version, the FK3, were built. It failed to be a serious rival to the B.E.2c upon which they were originally based and most ended up in training units, although at least one Royal Flying Corps squadron on active service was equipped with the type.

Armament

Designed at a time when there was little difference between a military and sporting aeroplane, and when the duties of a military aeroplane were unclear, the B.E.1 and B.E.2 were intended to be efficient flying machines. No thought was given to them being armed, nor was it considered that their role would ever require it.

At the outbreak of war, aeroplanes of both sides flew reconnaissance and observation missions unarmed, and if by chance another aeroplane was seen, crews would wave to each other in a friendly fashion. But such gentlemanly conduct could not last for long and observers began to take pistols and rifles with them to take aim at an enemy aeroplane

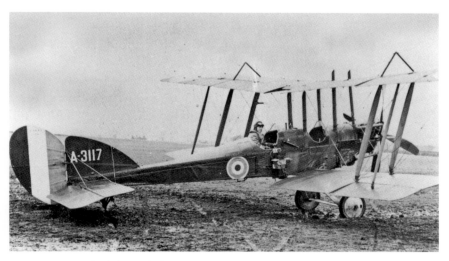

A3117, a B.E.2e built by Wolseley Motors, showing the cumbersome camera installation common to such machines.

B.E.2c, 2687, with bomb racks under its lower wings.

that came within range. The observer in the B.E.2 had been placed, as was common practice, in the forward cockpit at the centre of gravity so that the machine's trim was unaffected were it to be flown solo. This position, surrounded by struts and wires with the propeller in front and wings to each side above and below, restricted his field of fire. It was therefore normal for the pilot to position his aeroplane so that the enemy machine was to his forward quarter where his observer had the best chance of a well-aimed shot. Even so, it was by no means uncommon for the observer to hit a part of his own machine.

The B.E.2's first aggressive role was as a bomber in which capacity it was usual to carry either four 20 lbs bombs in racks under the lower wings or a 112 lbs bomb in a cradle beneath the fuselage. The bomb release was achieved by pulling a cable. If the machine was flown solo, a greater weight of bombs could be carried, especially if the range was short and the petrol tanks did not need to be completely filled. An accurate and dependable bombsight had yet to be devised, and the accuracy of the bombing depended as much upon luck as the skill of the pilot.

Armaments intended for use against balloons and airships included Le Prieur rockets which were fired electrically from tubes fitted to the outer interplane struts. Aiming was mostly down to luck but a number of observation balloons were destroyed. Efforts to mount a machine

An unidentified B.E.2c with an unusual arrangement of two sets of bomb racks under the fuselage. The exhaust pipes are also of an unusual design.

gun began after the introduction of the B.E.2c whose more powerful engine allowed additional weight to be carried. The gun chosen was the American-designed Lewis that weighed about 27 lbs not including the ammunition drum that held fifty rounds. The first mounting comprised a bracket on the fuselage side carrying a socket into which a pin, clamped to the gun at its centre of gravity, was placed so that the gun could be swivelled as needed to take aim. This was known colloquially as the candlestick mounting and appears to have been created, ad hoc, by squadron mechanics. This device allowed the user to fire both forwards and backwards, and gave a reasonable field of fire albeit at the risk of hitting his own machine.

The first official design for a gun mount, the No. 1 Mk.1, was a modified version of the same concept, but placed the mount on a front centre section strut and afforded both elevation and traverse. A modified version that could be folded flat against the fuselage side when not in use was designated No. 1 Mk.2. In either case, only one gun was normally carried and the observer was expected to move it from one side to the other as demanded. The candlestick mount was also occasionally fitted

A young airman demonstrates how the No. 1 gun mount gave a field of fire to the side and obliquely forwards. The machine is also provided with a Strange mounting between the cockpits.

This crashed B.E.2c has a Lewis gun on No. 1 Mk.1 mounts on each side of the fuselage although they could not have been fired in such a position without hitting the propeller. Bomb release toggles are also fitted conveniently to the pilot's right hand.

further back, allowing the pilot to use the gun when the machine was flown solo, the gun muzzle often being secured by wires to give a fixed line of fire. Similarly, the No. 1 mount, if fixed to the rear centre section strut, could be used by the pilot to fire forwards within the limited field of fire available to him.

With No. 1 Mk.2 mounts on the rear centre section struts, bomb racks and Le Prieur rocket-launching tubes on the wing struts, this machine appears ready for anything its desert location can throw at it.

Despite their rather crude appearance, the gun mounts could be used to good effect. On 19 September 1915, 2nd Lt Harold Medlicott of 2 Squadron with 2nd Lt Gilbert as his observer, were carrying out an artillery observation near Lens when they spotted an enemy two-seater. They positioned themselves to attack opening fire with a Lewis gun on the left-hand mounting from 100 yards. After a full drum had been fired, the Albatros caught fire, but Gilbert fired a second drum to make sure. Medlicott seems to have attacked every enemy aircraft he saw and after several inconclusive combats with Lt Rice as his observer, scored again on 11 October with the front seat occupied by Lt Russel. Their victim was another Albatros two-seater that was shot down near Sailly-sue-Lys where the crew was taken prisoner. Medlicott also invented a mount in which the socket to carry the gun was attached to a bar between the front centre section struts and arranged so as to slide along as required. Thus a single gun could be fired to either forward quarter without the need to change mounts. This, although often referred to by the name of its creator, was officially designated gun mount No. 2 Mk.1. A wire guard was often used to restrict the travel of the gun's muzzle and so prevent the user shooting his own propeller. The No. 2 Mk.2 and Mk.3 were minor refinements of the original design and did not change its basic concept or improve its effectiveness.

This machine is provided with both a No. 1 gun mount, apparently for the pilot's use, and a No. 4 or Strange mounting for rearward defence.

Captain L. A. Strange of 12 Squadron invented what was probably the most sophisticated mount of all. This comprised a swivelling pillar fixed between the cockpits with a toothed quadrant allowing the gun to be held in place at various angles of elevation. It could be employed by the observer to fire to the rear or by the pilot to fire forwards with equal facility. This was officially adopted as the No. 4 Mk. 1 mount but was almost always referred to by its inventor's name.

The No. 10 Mk. 1 or 'Goalpost' was a frame fitted between the cockpits onto which the Lewis gun could be mounted to allow the observer, by turning in his seat or even kneeling on it, to fire directly to the rear. Since the muzzle of the gun was located over the pilot's head, it must have been rather disconcerting to use, but did provide an effective defence against an attack from above and behind.

Despite the wide choice of gun mounts available, a number of machines remained unarmed in front line service. With the exception of the No. 4 and later versions of No. 2, these machine gun mountings were noted as obsolete in a training manual issued in July 1916, but continued in service throughout the war.

An unidentified B.E.2c fitted with the No. 10 Mk.1 'Goalpost' gun mount that allowed the observer to fire to the rear or, by reversing the gun, the pilot to fire obliquely forwards. The exhaust pipes are of an unusual design. (*Peter Wright*)

The ideal solution to arming an aeroplane, especially one flown solo, was to fix the machine gun to the front. However, the problem in a tractor design was to prevent bullets from hitting the propeller and pusher aeroplanes were deemed too slow to catch their prey. In the spring of 1915, a bizarre effort was made to combine the aerodynamic efficiency of a tractor design with the forward field of fire afforded by a pusher. Drawings were completed in June and a modification of B.E.2c, 1700, commenced. The observer's cockpit was eliminated and the engine moved back, positioning the propeller fifteen inches ahead of the upper wing. The centre section struts were splayed outwards to clear the engine cylinder, a new broader centre section increasing the span to over forty feet. A plywood nacelle to house the observer was mounted on an extension of the propeller shaft, supported by struts added to the undercarriage and braced by wires to prevent it rotating.

Modifications were completed by 13 August and the modified B.E.2c, now designated B.E.9, was flown to Netheravon for service evaluation on 25 August. The forward view was considered 'excellent' and the field of fire 'better than any other seen here'. It was, however, criticised for its lack

This B.E.2e has extensive racks for Lewis gun ammunition drums located outside the cockpits and appears to have a gun mounting on the upper centre section where it would fire clear of the propeller, but would be all but impossible to reload.

A 15 Squadron B.E.2c in the Middle East. The front cockpit has been covered and the pilot's cockpit fitted with extensive armour against retaliatory small arms fire while bombing troops on the ground.

The ingenious B.E.9, despite many favourable reports, failed to provide a viable solution to the problem of providing a forward-firing gun.

of dual control and on 31 August returned to the Royal Aircraft Factory for this to be provided. On 11 September, it was flown to France so that front line pilots and observers could operate it and offer their opinions. It spent time with several different squadrons, was flown over the lines and on 13 October, engaged in a brief and inconclusive encounter with a enemy machine while being flown by Lt Glen of 8 Squadron.

Reviews were at best mixed. The forward view and field of fire were generally praised but the lack of communication between the crew was seen as a problem. So, too, was the observer's prospect for survival in the event of a landing on its nose as the B.E.2c was prone to do so on soft ground. The adoption was not recommended and the aeroplane returned to Farnborough on 9 January 1916. Although it now appears remarkable that no attempt was made to reverse the crew positions to place the observer in the back seat where he would have a clear field of fire against an attack from the rear, there was no superior substitute for what was already in use. Such a move would not have significantly improved the observers field of fire to the rear – at least until the invention of the synchronisation gear to allow a gun to fire forwards through the propeller disc – and rendered the machine virtually defenceless against a foe dead ahead.

Fokker Fodder

In the summer of 1915, the solution to effectively arming an aeroplane was finally found in the invention of a device that would prevent the gun firing whenever a propeller blade was in a bullet's path. This, it was realised, could be achieved by fitting a cam to the propeller shaft that would control the firing mechanism and stop the gun firing as the propeller blade came in line with the gun's muzzle.

Although both the British and French had made abortive attempts to create such a device, it was the Dutchman, Antony Fokker, who first perfected it and was working for Germany. Fortunately for the Allies, the new monoplane, fitted with its deadly forward-firing machine gun, was brought into service in very small numbers spread along the whole front. It proved to be highly effective as Allied pilots initially believed that they were safe from attack when the enemy was behind them. Before Fokker's invention, aircrew casualties had been largely caused by ground fire, both anti-aircraft and small arms or mechanical failure. Air combat losses were now a danger, and although the number of machines lost in combat remained small, it created a considerable stir amongst the Allies. The press began to write about the 'Fokker Scourge' and the British crews, with their grim humour, considered themselves and their machines to be 'Fokker Fodder'.

The pilots of the new German fighters became national heroes, their successes and combat scores reported in the national newspapers. First among them was Max Immelman who became known as 'The Eagle of Lille' followed by Oswald Boelcke who wrote the rules of air combat for future pilots to follow. On 5 January 1916, Boelcke spotted two B.E.2cs from 2 Squadron and closed in hoping for his seventh victory that would bring his score level with Immelman's. He attacked the rearmost machine,

Above: The Fokker monoplane with its forward-firing Maschinengewehr 08 'Spandau' machine gun was no sight a B.E.2 crew wished to see.

Right: Oberleutnant Max Immelmann, 'The Eagle of Lille', wearing the Pour le Merite (Blue Max) around his neck. He was the first of the Fokker aces.

1734, damaging its controls and wounding both 2nd Lt W. E. Somervill and Lt G. C. Formilli, so causing the machine to crash. Boelcke visited his victims in hospital, bringing them newspapers and a photograph of their crashed machine.

Although taken as a percentage of the number in service – several other types of machines suffered higher losses – crews of the B.E.2 seemed particularly vulnerable as it was the type in service in the greatest numbers and its occupants spent their time in action observing enemy movements than searching the skies for enemy fighters.

B.E.2c, 2039, that
was shot down by
a Fokker on 29
December 1915.

However, the latest enemy machines were not invincible nor their pilots always keen to engage in combat once the initial element of surprise had been lost. An alert crew had a good chance of fending off an attack as the following extract from the official weekly summary of the Royal Flying Corp's work in the field, known affectionately as 'Comic Cuts', shows:

> RFC Communiqué No.20 – 11th November 1915
>
> 2nd Lt. Allcock and 1 AM Bowes, 2 Sqn in a B.E.2c escort to a reconnaissance machine, were attacked by a Fokker which dived underneath them opening fire at 300 ft. range. Lt Allcock turned and from the back mounting fired half a drum at the Fokker which cleared off.

As well as the single-seat Fokkers, the new German two-seat Albatros and Aviatik aeroplanes had to be feared. With their observers who had now moved to the rear cockpit and armed with a swivel-mounted machine gun, these aeroplanes could be flown quite aggressively when the occasion demanded.

Naturally, the Royal Flying Corps would have liked to be equipped with an aeroplane better designed for fighting, and in the autumn of 1915, requested that they be provided with a two-seat machine that was capable of defending itself. However, they accepted that until such a machine was available, they would have to carry on and do their best

Above left: Hauptmann Oswald Boelcke wearing the Blue Max.

Above right: 1734 was shot down by Oswald Boelcke on 5 January 1916. The crew, although both wounded, became prisoners of war.

with what they had. Orders were therefore given that machines on reconnaissance missions should be escorted, albeit by other aeroplanes of the same poorly-armed type. Critics suggested that the escort machines were more of a sacrifice than a benefit. One such critic was C. G. Grey, editor of *The Aeroplane* magazine, who had long been opposed to the very existence of the Royal Aircraft Factory. Grey frequently voiced his opinion that aircraft design and manufacture should be left entirely in the hands of private enterprise (which placed advertisements in his magazine where the Factory did not) who were typically quick to condemn the B.E.2c.

A more outspoken critic was Noel Pemberton Billing. Born in 1881, Billing was an adventurer as colourful as the heroes of popular fiction. He ran away to sea at the age of fourteen, ended up in South Africa and, still underage, joined the Natal Mounted Police. He fought and was twice wounded in the Boer War after which he returned to England and opened a petrol station at Kingston-on-Thames. Well before its time, it failed as many of his business ventures would and he returned to South Africa for a while. In 1909, he attempted to launch an aviation colony at Fambridge in Essex, but this too was premature and failed to attract sufficient interest to make it viable. Billing's interest in aviation continued and in 1913 he bet Frederick Handley Page that he could obtain his pilot's wings on the same day that he first sat in an aeroplane.

Noel Pemberton Billing MP who openly
accused the Royal Flying Corps of murder.
(*Colin Huston*)

Handley Page accepted the bet and Billing, starting his first lesson just
after dawn, passed the simple test before breakfast. Billing founded a
company making seaplanes and, he reasoned, since a craft that operated
on and under the water was a submarine, one that operated on and over
the water should be 'supermarine'. The legendary name was therefore
born and he later sold the company to his works manager, Mr Scott-
Paine.

At the outbreak of war, Billing joined the Royal Navy Air Service
and was involved in planning the famous bombing raid on the airship
sheds at Friedrichshafen on Lake Constance. Billing was to later resign
his commission in order to stand for Parliament as an independent.
Although defeated on his first attempt at Mile End on 10 March 1916,
he won the seat for East Hertfordshire, styling himself as the first 'Air
Member' although several existing MPs had debated knowledgeably on
aeronautical matters for some years previously.

Billing was not long in making his presence felt and, during a debate
on the air services on 22 March, made a long and accusatory speech
condemning the administration of the Royal Flying Corps. He called
for the amalgamation of the two separate air services into a single force
during which he shocked the house with the following statement:

> I do not intend to deal with the colossal blunders of the Royal Flying Corps,
> but I might refer briefly to the hundreds, nay thousands, of machines which

they have ordered, and which have been referred to by our pilots at the front as Fokker Fodder with regard to which every one of our pilots when he stepped into them if he got back it would be more by luck and his own skill than any mechanical assistance he got from the people who provided him with the machine.

I do not wish to touch a dramatic note, but if I did I would suggest that a number of our gallant officers in the Royal Flying Corps had been rather murdered than killed.

Mr Tennant, Under Secretary of State for War, replying on behalf of the Government, explained that they were well aware of the situation and required no such language to make them realise the importance of the matter. He stated that the air services were efficient and doing good work, and that they were being expanded and updated as fast as the aeroplanes could be turned out. He concluded by stating that the word 'murder' ought not to have been used and that the application of it was untrue. Billing immediately rose to say:

> I repeat the statement, and if the hon. gentleman wishes to challenge that statement I will produce such evidence that will shock this house.

He sat down amidst a clamour of cries of 'Do it now!' and was challenged to produce his evidence. On 28 March, Billing responded to the challenge by stating that the Under Secretary for War should have made a '...dignified and complete denial of my charges, instead of replying to the one dramatic note struck on the question of our pilots being rather murdered than killed'. He continued by again stating that pilots were being asked to accomplish tasks of which their machines were incapable, adding the following statement:

> If the officials who were responsible for deciding the types of machines in which our officers were to take to the air failed either by ignorance, intrigue, or incompetence to provide them with the best machines that this country could produce they were guilty of a crime for which only a fastidious mind could fail to find a crime.

He then read out passages from a series of letters mostly from the fathers of young airmen complaining about engine failures, poorly sited

The observer's view to the rear. His Lewis gun, at the right of the picture, is fitted to an unusual and possibly homemade mounting.

aerodromes and the 'dud' aeroplanes they were obliged to fly while in training. He continued his attack upon the B.E.2c and its makeshift armament stating that:

> ...our machines are dispatched to France, in most cases, as aeroplanes only. On their arrival the local squadron smiths did their best to convert them into weapons of war. A gun is stuck here and a bomb is hung on there. The performance of the machine loses 10 to 20 per cent of its efficiency. For example the official speed of a B.E.2c was something less than eighty miles an hour. That in all conscience was low enough when that machine was called upon to fight a Fokker, or other German machine, with a speed of 110 miles an hour whereas by the time it had been turned into this travesty of a weapon of war its speed was reduced to about 68 miles an hour.

Billing then proceeded to read out a long list of pilots killed by engine failure, flying accidents and similar incidents including a few who had died in action. He asked the house to imagine being a pilot flying over enemy lines, unarmed and knowing that his machine was only capable of 72 mph, to be attacked by a faster aeroplane with two guns, one firing ahead and one astern. Billing asked them to picture how an observer must feel, flying at a height of up to 10,000 feet, with his pilot shot dead with the understanding that he must eventually crash to his death simply because the officials did not provide dual controls that might have saved his life. He concluded his speech by saying:

> It is frequently difficult even in law, to draw a hard and fast line between murder and manslaughter or, again, between manslaughter and an accident caused by criminal negligence. When this negligence was caused by the official folly of those in high places, coupled with entire ignorance of the technique which, in this instance, could alone preserve human life, official folly became criminal negligence, and when the death of a man ensued the line between such official folly and murder was purely a matter for a man's own conscience.

He sat down to cries of 'Hear, hear' and the debate continued to deal with other aspects of the nation's aerial defence including the poor provision of anti-aircraft guns against raiding Zeppelins.

B.E.2c, 2008, of 8 Squadron was shot down on 19 September 1915, probably by Hptm H. J. Buddecke. The pilot, 2nd Lt W. H. Nixon, was killed and his observer, Capt. J. Stott, wounded and taken prisoner.

Tennant, when he rose to respond, dealt first with the question of anti-aircraft guns before tackling Billing's accusation. He stated that the enemy's 'new trick' had given them a certain advantage. However, their tactics were now being adequately met and that reconnaissance, despite the difficult conditions, was being carried out entirely to the satisfaction of the Commander in Chief. He added that '...fighting in the air continued with no advantage to the enemy' and aeroplane research and manufacturing was rapidly increasing. After attempting to reassure the house that the situation was nowhere near as bad as painted by Billing and that the majority of aerial missions were completed without incident, Tennant went on to promise that he would ask the prime minister to set up an independent enquiry to investigate the matter.

Lt Gen. Sir David Henderson, who as Director General of Military Aeronautics was responsible for equipment and management of the Royal Flying Corps, had listened to the debate from the public gallery. He not only gave his full support to the enquiry but immediately offered Tennant his resignation, although this was refused until the result of the enquiry was known. On 30 March, the Army Council announced that a Committee of Enquiry would indeed be held:

> To enquire and report whether, within the resources placed by the War Office at the disposal of the Royal Aircraft Factory and the limits imposed by War Office orders, the organisation and management of the factory are efficient, and to give the Army Council the benefit of their suggestions on any points of the interior administration of the factory which seem to them capable of improvement.

The committee was to be chaired by Mr Richard Burbidge, General Manager and later Managing Director of the famous department store Harrods. Other members were Sir Charles Parsons, H. F. Donaldson and R. H. Griffith (Secretary). The Committee set to work with commendable dispatch and witnesses included Lt Gen. Sir David Henderson and members of his staff, Mervyn O'Gorman, Mr Heckstall Smith, Assistant Superintendent of the Royal Aircraft Factory, and various members of the Factory staff. Billing was far from satisfied and continued his campaign of complaints against the conduct of the aerial war. On 2 May, he again asked the house whether a decision had been made to not send further B.E.2cs to France. The inevitable reply was that there was no machine

Lt Kurt Wintgens examining the wreckage of a B.E.2c he shot down killing both the crew.

available that was superior to the B.E.2c although several were currently under development following a request the previous autumn by the Royal Flying Corp for a machine that could defend itself.

Eventually, Billing's pressure on the Government had the desired effect and a second Committee of Enquiry was announced, this time under the chairmanship of a high court judge, Sir Clement Bailhache. The enquiry was to examine the administration and command of the Royal Flying Corps with particular reference to charges made both in Parliament and elsewhere, and to make any recommendations for improvement.

Meanwhile, the Burbidge Committee completed its investigation into the efficiency of the Royal Aircraft Factory and on 12 May, published its report in which it recorded the functions, staffing levels and expenditure of the Royal Aircraft Factory. It noted that since the outbreak of war, the Factory had built a total of seventy-seven aeroplanes including experimental prototypes while private industry had to date supplied over 2,120.

The report also explained the process by which new designs were submitted, as a draft, for approval by the War Office before detailed drawings were prepared, the process taking from six to nine months from the original concept to the commencement of manufacture. The enquiry had found the administrative processes 'extremely elaborate'

B.E.2e, 5821, appears to be awaiting an inspection of some description. The aeroplane in the background is a Sopwith 1½ Strutter.

and recorded that delays to production had occurred due to occasional errors in drawings for which the Royal Aircraft Factory was responsible. In conclusion, the report stated that an experimental organisation such as the Royal Aircraft Factory was needed to exist and that the standards of efficiency required by the War Office was being met and noted:

> We do not consider that the competition of the Royal Aircraft Factory with the trade should, if reasonably administered, be the cause of any detrimental friction or trade feeling.

Also, the committee believed that salaries paid to senior staff were too low and went on to suggest ways in which it thought the Factory's output might be increased. This report, with the omission of certain figures that may have been valuable to the enemy, was published by His Majesty's Stationery Office as paper Cd8191, priced 1½d, on 19 July 1916. It seems doubtful that Billing would have been satisfied by it. Although no blame was attached to the Royal Aircraft Factory or its management, O'Gorman's contract as superintendent was not renewed. In late August 1916, O'Gorman left the company and was replaced on 21 September by Henry Fowler, formerly an engineer with Midland Railway. A number of senior staff also left, although whether out of loyalty to O'Gorman or in search of the higher salaries mentioned in the report is unclear.

Meanwhile, the judicial enquiry into the Royal Flying Corps held its first meeting at Westminster Hall on 16 May under the direction of its chairman, Mr Justice Bailhache. Other members present were Mr J. H. Balfour Browne, KC; Mr J. G. Butcher, KC, MP; Mr Edward Short, KC; Sir Charles Parsons, FRS (who had also been a member of the Burbidge Committee); Mr Charles Bright FRS; and Mr Cotes Preedy (Secretary). Little progress was made that day as Billing refused to attend as requested to present his allegations, including the charge of murder to the enquiry. As he explained in a lengthy letter to the press, his allegations had been made against the high command of both the Royal Flying Corps and Royal Naval Air Service and would therefore state his case to an enquiry into the Royal Flying Corps only. He also stated that he did not consider that a committee composed of a judge, three lawyers, a retired civil engineer and an expert on steam turbines could '...come to any useful conclusions on so technical a subject'. However, when the committee met the following week to hear evidence from other witnesses including Mr Joynson-Hicks MP who had been a critic of government policy on aviation for many years, Billing eventually turned up.

Joynson-Hicks stated that since the introduction of the Fokker, the Allies no longer possessed 'mastery of the air'. He also pointed out that official advice to pilots on how to meet the new foe included the words: 'The Fokker, when in action, seeks by exercise of its superior speed and climbing power, to obtain a position above its enemy.' He claimed that this proved that the Fokker was faster than the B.E.2c, a fact that had never been denied.

Lord Montague, who was interviewed on 11 June, began by saying that he considered the Royal Aircraft Factory to be wasteful and inefficient, but was interrupted by the chairman who reminded him that the enquiry was into the management of the Royal Flying Corps, not the Factory. However, Lord Montague continued by stating that pilfering by Factory staff was commonplace and an individual with 'big pockets' had stolen enough parts to build an engine. Lord Montague was again reminded by the chairman to adhere to evidence relative to the committee's terms of reference. A number of witnesses from the industry were also heard, one of whom, Mr Algernon Berriman, chief engineer at the Daimler Company, stated:

Another B.E.2c that was shot down and examined by German troops. The fate of the crew is not known.

> The RAF engine and the B.E.2c may have their defects, but they form a combination that has been instrumental in enabling the Royal Flying Corps to perform valuable service in France.

When finally called upon, Billing repeated his accusation that those responsible for providing aeroplanes to the Royal Flying Corps had failed, either by intrigue or incompetence, to provide the best machines available. He went on to give details of numerous cases in which pilots had died while flying the B.E.2. These included both the fatal crash of Edward Busk while test flying at Farnborough and that of Desmond Arthur in 1913 due to a faulty repair. He attempted to read out a letter from the father of a pilot killed while flying at Gallipoli, but was stopped when it was pointed out that the Royal Flying Corps did not operate in the Dardanelles and the aeroplane must have been a navy machine and therefore outside the scope of the enquiry. Billing's evidence, much of it equally irrelevant, continued for several days until members of the committee grew visibly tired of him. He appeared to be able to provide little or no hard evidence to support his accusations of intrigue or incompetence and presented each of his incidents with the assumption that, since the machine had crashed, it must have been faulty.

The committee sat through June and into July 1916 hearing evidence from fifty-four witnesses in public although information believed sensitive and of use to the enemy was taken in private. Deliberating upon the mass of statements took time and their final report was not made public until December. It dealt at length with the difficulties experienced in setting up a new branch of the armed forces and in foreseeing how it would develop and assessing what equipment would be needed and in what quantities. The Royal Aircraft Factory, the report stated, should be judged by its greatest achievement, the B.E.2c, which was aerodynamically sound and capable of being mass produced by companies that had never previously built aeroplanes. The report concluded:

> No one could complain if Mr Pemberton Billing had asked for these cases to
> be enquired into to ascertain whether the death of these men could have been
> prevented. But, based upon these incidents, a charge of criminal negligence, or
> of murder, is an abuse of language and entirely unjustified.

Thus the high command of the Royal Flying Corps was exonerated, although it was to be merely a temporary reprieve. Public reaction to aerial attacks on London the following summer led to further enquiries into the management and operation of both The Royal Flying Corps and Royal Navy Air Service, and their amalgamation from 1 April 1918 into a single service, the Royal Air Force. Cleared of any blame but with its reputation tarnished by the accusations made about it, the B.E.2 remained in production and service. Its greatest trial was yet to come.

Final Developments

Development of the B.E.2 continued and by October 1915, a new variant, the B.E.2d, had been developed incorporating dual controls. In order to accommodate the rudder cables and torque tube connecting the two control columns, the main petrol tank, which in earlier variants had been located under the observer's seat, was replaced by an additional tank in the decking between the cockpits and a blister-shaped gravity tank under the upper port wing. The capacity of the existing gravity tank in the decking behind the engine was increased from fourteen to nineteen gallons, bringing the overall capacity up from thirty-two to forty-one gallons, providing a useful increase in range and endurance. The rigging notes for the type included the provision of an additional six feet of shock cord to each wheel to cope with the additional weight of fuel. However, these changes had an adverse effect on the machine's unspectacular rate of climb, almost doubling the time taken to reach 6,000 feet. Although over 650 B.E.2ds were ordered, only a small number found their way to France, the majority serving with training units where their dual controls were an advantage and poor rate of climb no great handicap.

Research indicated that under extreme conditions the existing fin might be of insufficient area to prevent an involuntary spin developing. Most pilots held this manoeuvre in dread as the recovery procedure, although simple, was not then on the syllabus at flight training schools. Experiments were conducted with a number of fins of increased area, these experiments later being fully described in a confidential paper presented by O'Gorman to the Advisory Committee for Aeronautics. B.E.2c, 1688, which was retained at Farnborough as a test vehicle, was fitted with several experimental fins of differing surface areas to evaluate their effect and the most effective selected.

The B.E.2d had a gravity tank installed under the port wing to make up for the omission of the tank under the observer's seat so that dual controls could be fitted.

In January 1916, B.E.2c, 2026, was fitted with the proposed new fin having a curved leading edge that increased its surface area from five square feet to eight and was sent to the Depot at St Omer for evaluation. Service pilots confirmed that it improved directional control and, most importantly, helped prevent incipient spins. The new fin was therefore adopted and fitted to all machines completed from then on as well as many that were in service. 2026 served with 12 Squadron, but on 16 May, crashed while landing and although repaired was not considered fit for further service and was returned to England to serve as a trainer.

The employment of the B.E.2c in a ground attack role, especially during the Battle of the Somme, inevitably led to aircraft being lost to small arms fire from the ground. Perhaps to avoid further accusations that crews were being sent to war in inadequate aeroplanes, a scheme was devised where the forward fuselage was fitted with sheet steel armour plate from the nose to the rear of the pilot's cockpit. The slab-sided armour, which did nothing to improve the machine's streamlining, weighed around 440 lbs and seriously handicapped the machine's performance. Nonetheless, at least fifteen machines were fitted with the armour and saw service on the Western Front. 2028, which had originally been built by Sir Armstrong, Whitworth & Co. Ltd., was with 6 Squadron by 9 September 1916 as an armoured machine. 2122 went to 8 Squadron and at least one example served with 15 Squadron,

A B.E.2c fitted with armour plate to the forward fuselage as protection against small arms fire from the ground.

remaining in service until the spring of 1917 carrying out ground attack and special reconnaissance missions. Other examples known to have been fitted with armour include 2713-2716 and 4093.

Ongoing research at Farnborough revealed that wings with outwardly raked tips were, at the speeds at which aeroplanes then operated, considerably more efficient than any other wing tip shape. Similarly, it was known if wings were superimposed as in a biplane, each affected the efficiency of the other reducing lift and increasing induced drag. Yet the ideal arrangement, the monoplane, if employing the shallow aerofoil sections of the day, required so much additional bracing to maintain rigidity that any aerodynamic advantage was lost. The best compromise was to reduce the span of the lower wing, eliminating struts and wires, and to increase the span of the upper wings, bracing the overhang from kingposts.

A new variant, the B.E.2e, was designed with a new, smaller horizontal tail and with wings following the new arrangement, the span of the upper wing increased by four feet and that of the lower wing reduced by six feet. The wings were rigged at a constant angle of incidence without any washout as the new raked tips were thought sufficient to prevent wing tip stalling. The ply covering to the top and bottom of the fuselage was eliminated and wire bracing substituted. Some fuselage members were changed from ash to steel tube, principally to alleviate problems experienced in obtaining sufficient supplies of good quality ash.

In February 1916, B.E.2c, 4111, was test flown fitted with the new wings and the improvement in both speed and climb was quite dramatic. Lateral control was considered to be 'very much better' and landing 'more easy'. The prototype was first tested fitted with an experimental up-rated RAF1b engine, achieving a top speed of 97 mph, boosting expectations of its improved performance. Since it was decided that this engine was not to be put into production, 4111 was fitted with a standard production 90-hp RAF1a (No. 22971/WD1009). Thus powered, the B.E.2e was 10 mph faster than the B.E.2c and this, together with the improvements in handling, was more than sufficient to ensure that it was put into production as soon as possible. Not only were a total of 1,000 examples placed on order with various contractors, but instructions were given to those building the B.E.2c and B.E.2d to fit the improved wings and tailplane. However, when the completed machines were received, complications arose for it was realised that manufacturers were producing three different machines. All had the same wings and tail surfaces, and looked very similar, but each had a different fuselage. To simplify the matter, especially when it came to the ordering of spares,

The B.E.2e introduced a new and more efficient wing structure.

it was therefore decided that the designation B.E.2e would apply only to those machines built entirely to the new design. Those that had originally been ordered as B.E.2c with the original fuselage would be designated B.E.2f and those with the B.E.2d fuselage would be known as the B.E.2g. Around 200 of each variant were eventually produced. The new wings were viewed with some suspicion, pilots wrongly thinking them structural unsound and a rumour circulated that the extensions would be damaged by violent manoeuvres. Experience proved this to be untrue and confidence in the new type returned.

B.E.10 was designed to carry out similar duties to the B.E.2 and had a deeper fuselage built around a framework of steel tubes. Four were ordered from the British & Colonial Aeroplane Company, but the order was cancelled when it was decided to concentrate on the B.E.2c. B.E.11 never progressed beyond the concept stage and no details of it survive. B.E.12 was a high-speed, single-seat scout conceived in the summer of 1915 and created by the conversion of 1697, the last of a batch of Renault-powered B.E.2cs built by British & Colonial. It was fitted with an RAF4a engine, a twelve-cylinder development of the RAF1 design developing 140 hp, the modifications to the engine mounts and increased fuel tank capacity taking up space created by the elimination of the front cockpit. Its first flight was made on 28 July 1915 and production examples began

B.E.12 was a single-seater based on the B.E.2c with a more powerful engine.

The prototype Bristol Fighter, adopted as a replacement for the B.E.2 first flew, as seen here, fitted with B.E.2d wings.

to arrive in service by the beginning of 1916. Although as vulnerable as the B.E.2c upon which it was based, the B.E.12 did good work both on long-range reconnaissance missions and as a bomber. Some were fitted with a forward-firing machine gun once a suitable synchronisation gear had been developed but were never intended as fighters, the stability inherited from the B.E.2 reducing their speed of manoeuvre.

The B.E.12 was still in production when the B.E.2e was introduced and was also fitted with the new wings to become the B.E.12a, its performance being similarly improved. The B.E.2 even managed to contribute to its own replacement, both aeroplanes which eventually superseded the B.E.2c employed B.E.2c components in their original form. The Bristol F2a, from which the famous Bristol Fighter was developed, first flew on 9 September 1916 fitted with the wings of a B.E.2d. At the time, the company was building the wings under contract although purpose-designed wings were substituted before the type was fully developed for production.

Designed by John Kenworthy, the Royal Aircraft Factory's proposal for a B.E.2 replacement employed the same wings and horizontal tail surfaces as the B.E.2e, mated with a completely new fuselage and powered by the 140-hp RAF4a V12 engine. It was armed with a forward-firing machine gun, synchronised to fire through the propeller disc and with a swivel-mounted gun for the observer. It might easily have been

The Royal Aircraft Factory's R.E.8 that replaced the B.E.2 for corps work employed the same wings as the B.E.2e.

given a designation in the B.E. series but was named the Reconnaissance Experimental No. 8 or R.E.8. Over 4,000 were built, eventually replacing the B.E.2 for all front line duties in Europe.

A number of alternative engines were also fitted at various times to the B.E.2 series. Some Royal Navy Air Service machines were fitted with the Curtiss OX5, a water-cooled V8 of similar size and power to the RAF1a, the air scoop replaced by a neat curved cowling and a car-type frontal radiator to address engine cooling. Performance was similar to that of the standard B.E.2c. A few Royal Navy Air Service B.E.2s were fitted with the 75-hp inline six-cylinder Rolls-Royce 'Hawk', again with a frontal radiator. A number of B.E.2 fuselages were employed without wings or tail surfaces as airship cars.

Several B.E.2cs were fitted experimentally with examples of the Hispano-Suiza engine. Of alloy construction with its cylinders cast on blocks instead of individually as in previous designs, it developed 150 hp from a mass not dissimilar to that of the RAF1a. Daimler-built 2599 was tested with a Hispano engine in March 1916 and, the following month, flown to the Central Flying School at Upavon for evaluation. Reports on its performance were favourable, but production of the Hispano

A number of B.E.2cs, especially in service with the Royal Naval Air Service, were fitted with the 90-hp Curtiss OX5 engine.

A Royal Navy Air Service B.E.2e powered by a 75-hp Rolls-Royce 'Hawk' engine.

A non-rigid airship employing a B.E.2 fuselage as its car. The wheels have been removed and additional petrol storage added to the underside of the fuselage to increase its endurance.

Although the 150-hp Hispano-Suiza engine as in this experimental installation brought a welcome increase in performance, the engine remained in short supply and was reserved for fighters.

Adding a supercharger to the standard RAF1a engine improved performance but was not adopted for production. (*Crown Copyright*)

engine and developments thereof could never keep pace with demand. Its use was largely restricted to aeroplanes such as the S.E.5 and Sopwith Dolphin, which had been designed around it, and no alternative engine was available without major modification to their design. None were ever made available for such obsolescent designs as the B.E.2.

However, 2599 retained its Hispano engine for a while and was fitted with a number of alternative radiator installations to find the most effective method of cooling, before moving on to experiments with superchargers.

At least one example, 4122, was fitted with an experimental variable pitch propeller developed by the Royal Aircraft Factory. Although successful, it was not considered necessary at the time, especially in view of its weight and additional complications.

Soldiering On

Morale amongst the crews of B.E.2s was obviously affected by the suggestion, that they were being sent to their deaths, like lambs to the slaughter, in machines that were simply no longer up to the job. The reputation of the B.E.2 had been sullied by Billing's accusations of murder and, even after the enquiry found there to be no case to answer, confidence in it declined. However, although experienced pilots mocked the B.E.2, new and inadequately trained pilots found reassurance in its stability and forgiving handling characteristics.

An unidentified B.E.2c flying over the sheds on Jersey Brow to the north-west of Farnborough Common. The two B.E.2cs on the ground both have the enlarged fin introduced in 1916.

An unidentified B.E.2c over the trenches performing its everyday duties of reconnaissance and artillery observation.

The Royal Flying Corps employed fighting aeroplanes of its own such as the nimble DH2 and the Royal Aircraft Factory's formidable F.E.2. The latter shared its outer wings with the B.E.2, both of which came into service in effective numbers early in 1916, and the F.E.8 joined them later the same year. These were all pushers, but each carried forward-firing machine guns and, by carrying out offensive patrols behind the enemy lines, strove to prevent enemy machines from reaching the front. Thus by April 1916, almost as soon as Billing was making his accusations in Westminster, the 'Fokker Scourge' had been contained and the B.E.2s were largely able to carry out their duties largely unmolested.

These duties remained the same: reconnaissance, artillery observation, signalling corrections by wireless and aerial photography with a clumsy plate camera attached to the side of the fuselage. Bombing continued but was increasingly the responsibility of other machines that could carry more weight. However, it was during a bombing mission that a B.E.2c scored the following remarkable success:

Communiqué No.27 – 5th January 1916.

Lt. R. H. Le Brasseur (B.E.2c, 16 Squadron) while on a bombing expedition to Douai was attacked by a Fokker which approached from behind. The B.E.2c endeavoured to evade the hostile machine, but it was too fast, so Lt. Le Brasseur turned to attack it. One drum was fired at the German and while Lt. Le Brasseur was fitting a second drum the Fokker approached to within less than 50 yards. The B.E.2c then fired a few more shots, and the hostile machine went spinning down vertically. Lt. Le Brasseur was then attacked by a second Fokker, whereupon he dived and turning, empted the remainder of the drum at the enemy which also went spinning down vertically. The B.E.2c was much damaged by machine gun fire and made a forced landing at Bruay.

Reconnaissance work kept the squadrons busy in the run up to the Battle of the Somme on 1 July 1916. Although the Royal Flying Corps had expanded considerably by this time, the B.E.2c was the single most numerous type in active service, equipping twelve of twenty-seven squadrons. On the opening day, the B.E.2c crews provided reconnaissance work on the progress of the battle and as artillery observation as the British targeted enemy guns which were shelling advancing troops. The next day, a total of twenty-eight B.E.2cs from various squadrons took part in bombing raids on railways around Cambrai, Busigny and St Quentin to prevent the enemy sending troops and stores to the front. Busigny station was hit as was a train south of Aubigny au Bac, but the

B.E.2cs of 13 Squadron at Savy in 1916. The aeroplane nearest the camera is 2504. (*P. H. T. Green Collection*)

A downed B.E.2d behind enemy lines in December 1916. Bomb release toggles have been fitted between the rails intended to hold a camera. The pilot's seatbelt is hanging over the cockpit side, the Lewis gun is on its mounting and there appears to be a mirror fitted in the centre of the pilot's windscreen.

major success was at St Quentin where several regiments of troops were preparing to board trains. A bomb fell on a shed filled with ammunition causing a huge explosion that set fire to nearby wagons that were also loaded with ammunition. The train that was to carry troops to the front was destroyed with the loss of all equipment and many of the men panicked fleeing in all directions, almost 200 being killed or wounded.

The 1916 Lord Mayor's Show in London included a number of aircraft including a captured German LVG two-seater and a B.E.2c, serial 4545. Their fuselages were towed on their own wheels behind Royal Flying Corps Crossley Tenders with their fully-rigged wing cells following on trailers, also towed by tenders. Presumably this was intended to boost the morale of the civilian population who turned out in their thousands to watch the parade.

By the end of August, the Fokker monoplane had been withdrawn and replaced by new biplane fighters such as the first Albatros single-seater whose performance was much superior to any British machine in service at the beginning of September.

By the following spring, Germany, with its new fighters, had regained mastery of the air. Preparations for the Battle of Arras, which opened on 9 April, required additional reconnaissance and photography. This led to further heavy losses, not just amongst the now long outdated B.E.2, but across the whole range of types operated by the Royal Flying Corps. This period in 1917 was known as 'Bloody April' with 245 machines – a quarter of the RFC's operational strength – shot down with 319 pilots and observers killed or taken prisoner of war. Sixty B.E.2s were casualties during the offensive, clearly showing that a year after Billing's accusations the type was still widely used on operational duties. Other

A3168 became Manfred von Richthofen's forty-seventh victim, both of its crew being killed. It was just one of seventeen B.E.2s amongst his eighty combat victories. (*Bruce Robertson Collection*)

losses for the month include thirteen R.E.8s and eight Bristol Fighters as these more modern designs began to replace the ageing B.E.2. Fortunately, the same month saw the introduction of the S.E.5 fighter and this, together with the Sopwith Camel, slowly turned the tide in the favour of the Allies.

As numbers of Bristols and R.E.8s increased, along with the introduction of other types such as the Armstrong Whitworth FK8 corps/reconnaissance machine and DH4 bomber, the B.E.2 was finally phased out. Yet, even after it was no longer employed on front line duties, the B.E.2 remained in France for communication duties and as an aerial taxi.

Home Defence

For centuries, defence of the British Isles rested with the Royal Navy whose mighty warships provided security from invasion for almost a thousand years. Therefore, when threatened with attack from the air, it naturally fell to the Navy to provide an adequate defence. However, after a number of Zeppelin bombing raids, although causing only minimal damage and few casualties, public outcry was such that action had to be taken. (Hence the experiments with the Airship Plane as described earlier.) On 7 June 1915, Flt Sub Lt R. A. Warneford managed to destroy a Zeppelin by dropping a bomb on it. The action took place over Belgium and while Warneford was awarded the Victoria Cross for his action, the public appeared not to recognise this as defending the British Isles from the dreaded Zeppelin menace. Therefore in February 1916, the Royal Flying Corps established a chain of Home Defence stations from which they could protect London and the East coast.

For flying and landing at night, the stable B.E.2c found a role for which it might have been created. It became the most numerous type employed against Zeppelins, its only drawback was that it took almost an hour for the B.E.2c to reach 10,000 feet, the height at which the enemy airships operated. A system of standing patrols was introduced with aeroplanes sent up in anticipation whenever the conditions seemed favourable for the raiders to attack.

In this new role, the B.E.2c was usually flown solo with additional petrol taking place of the observer, its ceiling slowly increasing as this was used up. Cockpit lighting was provided so that the pilot could read his instruments. The usual armament was a Lewis gun loaded with incendiary ammunition with which to set light to the hydrogen that provided airships with their lifting power. The use of such ammunition

One of several designs of postcards that were widely sold to commemorate the destruction of the raiding German airships. That the aeroplane looks nothing like a B.E.2c did not detract from sales.

was banned by the rules of war for use against personnel. It was therefore usual for pilots to carry written orders stating that the ammunition was only to be fired at the gasbag.

The first success came on the night of 31 March/1 April when 2nd Lt Alfred de Brandon, flying a B.E.2c from Hainault Farm near Romford in Essex, encountered LZ15. It had already been hit by anti-aircraft fire and was losing gas, and with it, height. De Brandon's attack made no visible difference to the Zeppelin, but it came down in the sea on its return. Unfortunately, on the same night, L22, which had set out to raid the London area, drifted to the north and therefore bombed Grimsby Docks. A bomb fell on a church hall near Cleethorpes seafront in which troops of the Manchester Regiment were billeted. The resulting explosion caused a great number of casualties and it was this rather than the demise of LZ15 that dominated the next day's news.

On the night of 2/3 September, Lt William Leefe-Robinson of 39 Squadron took-off from Sutton's Farm to the east of London to patrol across the Thames in a B.E.2c, believed to have been 2693, with his ammunition drums loaded with a combination of tracer and incendiary rounds. The action which followed is best described in his own words:

To the Officer Commanding No.39 Home Defence Squadron.

Sir,

I have the honour to make the following report on night patrol made by me on the night of the 2/3 instant. I went up at about 11.08 pm on the night of the 2nd with instructions to patrol between Sutton's Farm and Joyce Green.

I climbed to 10,000 feet in 53 minutes. I counted what I thought were ten sets of flares – there were a few clouds below me, but on the whole it was a beautifully clear night. I saw nothing until 1.10 am when two searchlights picked up a Zeppelin S.E. of Woolwich. The clouds had collected in this quarter and the searchlights had some difficulty in keeping on the airship. By this time I had managed to climb to 12,000 feet and I made in the direction of the Zeppelin – which was being fired on by a few anti-aircraft guns – hoping to cut it off on its way eastward. I slowly gained on it for about ten minutes. I judged it to be about 800 feet below me and I sacrificed some speed in order to keep the height. It went behind some clouds, avoiding the searchlight and I lost sight of it. After about 15 minutes of fruitless search I returned to my patrol.

I managed to pick up and distinguish my flares again. At about 1.50 am I noticed a red glow in the N.E of London. Taking it to be an outbreak of fire, I went in that direction. At 2.05 am a Zeppelin was picked up by searchlights over N.N.E London (as far as I could judge).

Remembering my last failure, I sacrificed height (I was at about 12,900 feet) for speed and nosed down in the direction of the Zeppelin. I saw shells bursting and night tracers flying around it. When I drew closer I noticed that the anti-aircraft aim was too high or too low, also a good many shells burst about 800 feet behind – a few tracers went right over. I could hear the bursts when about 3,000 feet from the Zeppelin. I flew about 800 feet below it from bow to stern and distributed one drum along it (alternate New Brock and Pomeroy). It seemed to have no effect, I therefore moved to one side and gave them another drum along the side – also without effect. I then got behind it and by this time I was very close – 500 feet or less below, and concentrated one drum on one part (underneath rear). I was then at a height of 11,500 feet when attacking the Zeppelin.

I had hardly finished the drum before I saw the part fired at glow. In a few seconds the whole rear part was blazing. When the third drum was fired there were no searchlights on the Zeppelin, and no anti-aircraft was firing. I quickly got out of the way of the falling, blazing Zeppelin and, being very excited, fired off a few Very lights, and dropped a parachute flare.

Having little oil or petrol left, I returned to Sutton's Farm, landing at 2.45 am. On landing I found that the Zeppelin gunners had shot away the machine

Left: Lt William Leefe-Robinson VC who shot down SL 11.

Below: Cockpit of Leefe-Robinson's B.E.2c showing the instrument board and switches for the cockpit lights. The external switch is for the ignition. The gun is fitted on the Strange mount ahead of the cockpit.

gun wire guard, the rear part of my centre section, and had pierced the main spar several times.

I have the honour to be, sir,

Your obedient servant,

W. Leefe-Robinson, Lieutenant, R.F.C.

The airship destroyed was the wooden-framed Schütte-Lanz SL 11 operated by the German Army that came down near Cuffley in Hertfordshire, its fall in flames visible across a wide area. Leefe-Robinson was fêted as a hero and was awarded a Victoria Cross for his courage in

Lt Frederick Sowery (second from right) with B.E.2c, 4112, in which he shot down Zeppelin L32.

pressing home his attack not only in the face of defensive fire from the airship, but also in accepting the very real risk of being hit by his own side's anti-aircraft fire.

Some three weeks later on 24 September, 39 Squadron scored again when 2nd Lt Frederick Sowery, flying B.E.2c, 4112, shot down Zeppelin L32 near Billericay in Essex. The crash site became a popular tourist attraction, a small admission fee being charged to raise funds for the Red Cross. Then, on 1 October, 2nd Lt Wulstan J. Tempest, flying 4577, shot down L31 over Potter's Bar. Tempest crashed on landing at Sutton's Farm writing off his mount, although fortunately without serious injury to himself.

A pilot from 36 Squadron, 2nd Lt I. V. Pyott, flying B.E.2c, 2738, from Seaton Carew, shot down L34 over the mouth of the Tees on 1 October 1916. The following evening, L21 was attacked three times by B.E.2cs from the Royal Navy Air Service, Yarmouth. First to encounter the airship was Flt Lt Egbert Cadbury in B.E.2c, 8625, followed by Flt Sub Lt G. W. R. Pare, and finally by Flt Sub Lt E. L. Pulling to whom the victory was officially credited, although all three pilots had no doubt contributed to the Zeppelin's destruction. L21 came down in the sea near Lowestoft. Before the year was out, 2nd Lt Alfred de Brandon, who had attacked LZ15 back in March, shot down L33.

ZEPPELIN BROUGHT DOWN IN FLAMES
AT CUFFLEY, NEAR ENFIELD, AT 2:30 A.M., SUNDAY SEPT 3rd 1916.
(DRAWN BY AN EYE-WITNESS)

Another postcard with an equally inaccurate artist's impression of the stricken airship SL 11. (*Colin Huston*)

Not only had public fears been calmed by the numerous successes, but Zeppelin raids were largely discontinued, losses having become too frequent while improved models were developed. The B.E.2cs had done good work and continued in action against night-raiding Gotha bombers until the summer of 1917. However, as new Zeppelin designs appeared that were able to operate at greater altitudes, other aeroplanes with superior ceilings and rates of climb were employed as night fighters. But the B.E.2c had a final victory on the night of 17 June 1917 when B.E.12, 6610, of 37 Squadron, flown by Lt L. P. Watkins, shot down L48 at Holly Tree Farm, Theberon, Suffolk. L48 was the last airship to fall on British soil during the war.

Training

Established in 1912, the Central Flying School was intended not to teach men how to fly, but to provide training in military aviation to members of the Royal Flying Corps who had at their own expense obtained a pilot's certificate. It therefore needed to be equipped with examples of the aircraft types found on active service such as the B.E.2, Maurice Farmans and Avros. At least ten B.E.2a aeroplanes were delivered to the Upavon site before the end of 1913, with more arriving the following spring.

When a number of flying training schools were established, almost all had the B.E.2 on strength. Initially, these were employed as examples of the type of machines pilots might expect to fly on active service. Later,

A pre-war line-up of aircraft, mostly B.E.2as at the Central Flying School.

This B.E.2e of 35 (Training) Squadron at Port Meadow shows the more colourful markings accepted at training units.

In training, crashes were common as novice pilots learned their craft and this B.E.2e managed to damage the roof of a cottage near its base at Montrose. The pilot is believed to have been unhurt.

B.E.2c, 8423, after a landing accident at Royal Navy Air Service, Cranwell, on 14 February 1917. The machine was not repaired.

A group of B.E.2s at the Wireless Experimental Establishment, Biggin Hill, in 1918. The machine nearest the camera is C7001.

B.E.2e, A2885, with 42 Training Squadron at Hounslow. The method of applying the serial is unusual.

when the B.E.2 was superseded by more advanced designs, it remained a useful step between basic trainers such as the Maurice Farman, on which pilots first flew solo, and the more powerful service types they might expect to fly in France. It was, of course, perfect for cross-country flying and for building up experience and confidence before moving on to other machines. At first, instructional machines served on the Western Front before being relegated to training, but the type's use in action finally diminished, production machines were delivered straight to flying training units.

There were only a few Royal Flying Corps and Royal Navy Air Service pilots during the First World War who had not flown the B.E.2 at some stage in their careers.

The flying training course included instruction in a variety of related subjects such as map reading and wireless use as well as lectures on the construction, rigging and maintenance of an aeroplane. The model chosen on which to base these lectures was almost inevitably the B.E.2.

Foreign Fields

In addition to its wide-scale deployment on the Western Front, the B.E.2 saw active service with the Royal Flying Corps in theatres of war around the globe. Both 14 and 17 Squadrons operated the type in Egypt, 14 Squadron transferred its operations to Palestine and 17 Squadron to Mesopotamia. 26 Squadron flew the B.E.2c in East Africa and 31 Squadron operated the type on the North-West Frontier.

30 Squadron flew the B.E.2c in Mesopotamia, and when General Townshend was besieged by the Turks in the town of Al-Kut on a loop in the Tigris river, flew food and supplies to the British troops. Flown solo,

B.E.2es above Abu Sueir.

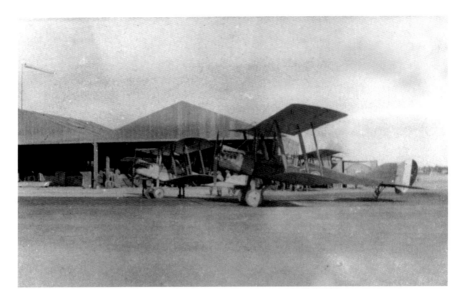

Above: A B.E.2e, 1808, and B.E.2c in the background with 58 Squadron at Suez. (*P. H. T. Green collection*)

Left: An unidentified B.E.2e on the North West Frontier of India (now part of Pakistan) in 1918.

the B.E.2c could carry 50 lbs of bombs on each lower wing root and a further 50 lbs attached to the undercarriage. However, efforts to break through the Turkish forces to relieve the town failed and Townshend was finally forced to surrender.

The Royal Navy Air Service also employed most variants of the B.E.2, a total of over 300 being ordered by the Admiralty, built by various contractors. At least five B.E.2as were at Eastchurch pre-war and, after the outbreak of hostilities, the Naval Air Station at Dunkirk operated a number of Renault-powered B.E.2cs.

This B.E.2c somewhere in the desert has modified exhaust manifolds and external racks for Lewis gun ammunition drums. The Lewis gun is fitted to a Strange mount between the cockpits and bomb racks are fitted below the wings.

Royal Navy Air Service B.E.2c, 8336, at Eastchurch in 1917. (*P. H. T. Green Collection*)

B.E.2c, 8624, at Royal Navy Air Service that had been converted to a single-seater and fitted with a Lewis machine gun. The non-standard exhausts were fitted to a number of Royal Navy Air Service machines.

The Royal Navy Air Service also shipped B.E.2cs to the Dardanelles, employing them for bombing raids and took them to East Africa where they were operated successfully against German forces before handing them over to 26 Squadron for continued service.

They were also used by the Royal Navy Air Service and the Royal Flying Corps for anti-submarine patrols around England's coastal waters where their stability was a great asset. Flown solo to increase their endurance, the pilot could largely ignore the controls and concentrate on watching the sea.

Amongst other nations, Australia was an early customer of the B.E.2. Two B.E.2as formed part of the original equipment of Central Flying School at Point Cook near Melbourne when it opened in March 1914. At the time, its other aircraft were two Deperdussin monoplanes and a Bristol Boxkite bought in 1912. These two B.E.2as were ordered directly from the British & Colonial Aeroplane Company and, after some delay to their completion owing to a shortage of strainers for the wire bracing, were shipped on the SS *Hawkes Bay*, arriving in February 1914.

Two Royal Navy Air Service B.E.2s, 47 and 50. Both saw service at Dunkirk early in the war with 50 also going to the Dardenelles.

A Renault-powered B.E.2c with 2 Wing Royal Navy Air Service at Imbros, an island off the coast of Turkey.

B.E.2cs with the Royal Navy Air Service in East Africa. (*P. H. T. Green Collection*)

Royal Navy Air Service B.E.2, 1145, after a bad landing at Redcar in October 1916. (*P. H. T. Green Collection*)

A close-up of the crashed 1145. The bombs, which can be seen under the nose, were used against submarines. (*P. H. T. Green Collection*)

Unidentified B.E.2a at the flying school at Point Cook, Australia.

Both 236, built by Vickers, and 237, built by British & Colonial, were shipped to Point Cook late in 1914 after a period in service with the Royal Flying Corps. Once in Australia, however, the aeroplanes may only have served as instructional airframes. No. 1 (Aus) Squadron, formed at Point Cook, arrived in Egypt in April 1916 and was equipped with the B.E.2c, many of them being handed down from 17 Squadron Royal Flying Corps. In December the same year, the first B.E.2e was received and the squadron gradually re-equipped with the updated type. It also had at least one B.E.12 on strength at some time. No. 3 Squadron, which served in France from September 1917, had a single B.E.2e on strength as did No. 4 Squadron. No. 7 Squadron, a training unit, also operated both the B.E.2c and B.E.2e.

One B.E.2c was instrumental in earning Lt F. H. McNamara a Victoria Cross. On 20 March 1917, while serving with No. 1 Squadron in Palestine, McNamara was on a bombing mission in a Martinsyde G100 when he saw B.E.2c, 4479, forced to land in enemy-held territory. Although under heavy fire from advancing troops and wounded in the thigh, McNamara landed nearby and attempted to rescue the downed

Top: A B.E.2c in Belgian markings but still with its Royal Flying Corps serial, 4461, on the fin.

Middle: With the crew positions reversed, a gun ring over the rear cockpit and a Hispano-Suiza engine with a synchronised Vickers gun on the cowling above it, this unidentified B.E.2c is typical of those in the Belgian Air Service.

Bottom: A Hispano-Suiza-powered B.E.2c of the Belgian Air Service shot down on 6 April 1917, apparently being examined or dismantled by German troops.

pilot on the wing of his Martinsyde. The machine turned over in the attempt to take-off and they abandoned it. They managed to start the engine of the damaged B.E.2c, and despite one wheel without a tyre, managed to take-off. McNamara, although weak with the loss of blood from his wounds, managed to fly seventy miles back to base, the machine almost collapsing on landing.

Amongst others, 2636, 2695, 4095, 4097 and 4102 went to Belgium to equip the 6ème Escadrille of Aviation Militaire Belge. On arrival, they were fitted with 150-hp Hispano-Suiza engines with round frontal radiators and neat circular cowlings. The crew positions were reversed and the side of the rear cockpit modified so as to be fitted with a Lewis gun on a French Eteve mounting ring. Some later examples had the cockpit sides modified so that a British Scarff ring could be fitted.

At least one B.E.2a served at the Indian Flying School at Sitapur that opened in 1913. A total of twenty-two B.E.2es were shipped to Norway, some of which were fitted with skis to allow operation from snow-bound fields. At least one of these remained in service until 1928. Other examples, all ex-Royal Flying Corps, found their way into the air services of Estonia, Greece, Holland and South Africa.

After the War was Over

Once the war was over, the flying schools ceased to operate, the Royal Air Force rapidly contracted and there was no place for the B.E.2. Thousands were disposed of and scrapped, many being bought for a nominal sum by people who wanted parts for other purposes. Wheels were fitted to wagons and trailers, wings became fences and the roofs of sheds. Only a handful remained in operation when the peace treaty was signed.

The last ever B.E.2b, A376, which was assembled from spares during 1916, was still extant at Farnborough in 1919, although what function it might have served is unknown. B.E.2c, 4550, had been used at the Factory – renamed as the Royal Aircraft Establishment in 1918 to avoid a clash of initials with the newly-created Royal Air Force – for testing air brakes in 1916. Thereafter, it was used for experiments with gyroscopes and remained in service after the war. In 1919, it took part in spinning trials and survived at least until 1924.

The 1921 RAF display at Hendon featured a machine described as the B.E.2xyz. It was a B.E.2c rigged with reduced stagger, fitted with a dummy ship funnel, from which smoke was somehow made to emerge, and an additional undercarriage above the centre section 'for inverted landings'. The modifications cannot have affected its performance much as their appearance suggests as it apparently flew a circuit during the display.

A total of eleven B.E.2es and a single B.E.2c, bought at disposal sales, appeared on the civil register. Most were used for joyriding although one, G-EAQR, was used for pleasure flying by its owner, Mr Wigglesworth of Canterbury, at least until 1921. The Royal Aero Club introduced a hire scheme for members, its fleet, all donated by the Aircraft Disposal

The so-called B.E.2xyz (then G-EAHS) at the RAF pageant at Hendon in 1921.

B.E.2e, G-EANW, sometime in the 1920s. (*Flight Photograph*)

B.E.2e G-EAVS with what appears to be a racing number on its rudder.

Company of Croydon, comprising three Avros, two Armstrong Whitworths and a B.E.2e. Charges were three pounds an hour for all types but the scheme was short lived.

Remarkably, the B.E.2e took part in a number of races. In 1921, one was entered in the First Croydon Handicap for aeroplanes with speeds under 100 mph, but perhaps the handicaps were over-optimistic about its performance as it was unplaced. A similar entry in the Second Croydon Handicap, flown by Mark Kerr, managed second place.

Neville Vincent flew a B.E.2 in the Club Handicap at Croydon on Easter Monday in 1922, but he too was unplaced, although he deserves praise for trying. A B.E.2e was originally entered for the 1925 Light Aeroplane Competition held at Lympe, but problems with its Certificate of Airworthiness prevented it taking part. In Australia, two B.E.2es found their way onto the civil register. C6986 became G-AUBF and later VH-UBF, and C7198 became VH-UBB. The former machine was later bought for £450 from Charles Knight, a Longreach stock and station agent, and became one of the first aeroplanes operated by Queensland and Northern Territories Aerial Service Company now known, more simply, as Qantas.

The B.E.2 Today

Five original B.E.2s survive to this day, as well as a number of reproduction machines, in various museum collections around the world. The reproductions include a B.E.2a under construction near Melbourne, Australia, intended to represent one of the machines in service with that country. A B.E.2b, painted to represent the machine flown by Rhodes-Moorhouse, is displayed in the Royal Air Force Museum at Hendon. This machine was built specifically for the museum by John Mackenzie.

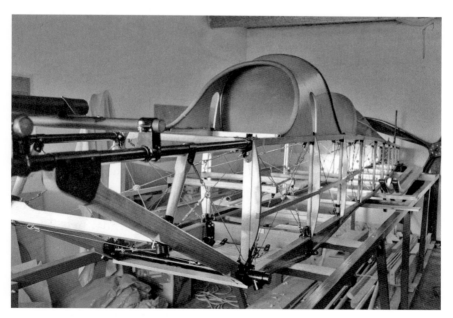

A B.E.2a reproduction fuselage under construction in Australia. Built to original drawings in 2012, it remains faithful to de Havilland's original design. (*Andrew Willox*)

Another view of the reproduction B.E.2a with the propeller fitted to give a sense of scale. (*Andrew Willox*)

Reproduction B.E.2b built by volunteers at Boscombe Down for display in a local museum and painted to represent the first aeroplane stationed there. (*Peter Olding*)

Another reproduction B.E.2b is owned by the Boscombe Down Aviation Collection, having been built to represent the first aeroplane to land on the airfield. The United States Army Aviation Museum at Fort Rucker, Alabama, has a reproduction B.E.2c believed to have originally been built by Gerald Burr in Canada. Another reproduction B.E.2c is displayed by the Yorkshire Air Museum at Elvington near York. This was originally built during the 1960s by RAF apprentices for display in the Royal Tournament and, although a fair facsimile of the type, its internal construction is not completely accurate.

The Militaire Luchvaartmuseum in Soesterberg, Netherlands, has a reproduction B.E.2c representing a machine in the service of that country while examples of both early and late model B.E.2cs are displayed at The Vintage Aviator Collection in New Zealand.

The original machines include B.E.2c, 2699, at the Imperial War Museum in London; B.E.2c, 9969, at the Musée de l'Air et Espace, le Bourget, Paris, France; B.E.2d, 5878, (originally believed erroneously to be 4112 in which Lt Sowery shot down L32, its true identity discovered during restoration) at the Canada Aviation and Space Museum in Ottawa.

Top: Reproduction B.E.2b on display at The Royal Air Force Museum, Hendon, painted to represent the machine flown by 2nd Lt W. Rhodes-Moorhouse VC.

Middle: Reproduction B.E.2c on display at the United States Army Aviation Center of Excellence, Fort Rucker, Alabama.

Bottom: Reproduction B.E.2c built by RAF apprentices and displayed at the Yorkshire Air Museum.

Top: B.E.2c, 2699, preserved by the Imperial War Museum and seen on a rare outing in the open.

Middle: B.E.2c, 9969, now preserved at the Musée de l'Air in Paris, seen here at Detling in Royal Flying Corps service.

Bottom: B.E.2d, 5878, preserved in Canada after restoration. (*Canadian War Museum*)

Top: B.E.2e, A1380, which served with the Norwegian Air Force and is preserved in that country.

Middle: B.E.2e, A1325, which served with the Norwegian Air Force after restoration to flying condition by The Vintage Aviator Ltd. in New Zealand. It now performs regularly in flying displays. (*TVAL*)

Bottom: A1325 airborne over its home base at Masterton, New Zealand.

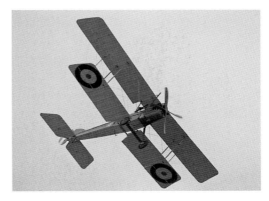

153

This reproduction B.E.2c, with the early skidded undercarriage, flies regularly in air shows at Masterton, New Zealand, where its pilots find it a delight to fly. (*Adrian Rumney*)

B.E.2e, 131, (ex-A1380) is displayed at Forsvarets Flysamling Museum at Gardermoen in Norway. B.E.2f, A1325, is located at New Zealand's Vintage Aviator Collection and has been restored to flying condition, performing regularly in air shows. Pilots who are accustomed to flying vintage aeroplanes, designed to operate from grass fields and to take-off and land directly into the wind, have found, as did their counterparts a century before, that it is pleasant and comfortable to fly.

Gene Demarco, who regularly flies both the original and reconstruction B.E.2, reports:

> I have become quite fond of the B.E.2c, it is a fine example of an early flying machine. In calm weather it is delightful and easy to fly.
>
> It is easy to see why early aviators called their flying machines kites; when you think about their light wing loading and large size these aeroplanes certainly feel more like kites being held aloft by the wind rather than machines using aerodynamics and a powerful engine to overcome the laws of physics.
>
> As a reconnaissance machine, the B.E.2 provided two seats and the ability to carry an observer or a camera, and in some cases a wireless. It was relatively easy to control and produced in large numbers. By far one of the simplest aircraft I have flown and one I immensely enjoy!

Perhaps with this in mind, we can finally forgive the B.E.2 for being vulnerable to a form of attack that it had never been designed to resist, and remember instead how well it performed its roles for which it had originally been intended.

Sources

The following sources were used in the preparation of this book:

Busk, E. T. (design notebook)
De Havilland, G. (flying logbook 1911-1913)
Farnborough Flight Log
Folland, H. (notebooks)
O'Gorman, M. J. P. (papers and diary)
RAE Museum Farnborough (now closed)

National Archive:

Files from AIR 1; AVIA 6; AVIA 14; CAB; and DSIR categories

Published Materials:

Advisory Committee for Aeronautics: 'Reports and Memoranda'
The Aeroplane magazine
Blackwoods magazine
Cross and Cockade International journal
Flight magazine
Hansard (record of Parliamentary debates)
The Morning Post newspaper
Royal Flying Corps Rigging Notes and training manuals
The Times newspaper
The War in the Air by Sir Walter Raleigh and H. A. Jones (Oxford University Press, 1922-1931)
WW1 Aero magazine

Index